D

Creative Christmas

Simple Crafts from Many Lands

Kathryn E. Shoemaker

Copyright © 1978 by Winston Press, Inc.
Library of Congress Catalog Card
Number: 78-59407
ISBN: 0-03-045716-5
Printed in the United States of America

Winston Press
430 Oak Grove
Minneapolis, Minnesota 55403

Dear Gentle Readers,

Christmas has always been my favorite celebration. As a child, I could hardly wait for December, and I never slept a wink on Christmas Eve. I still can't!

From the time when I was six years old, my mother let me have a small Christmas tree in my room to decorate. I covered that first tree with my collection of tiny stuffed animals and dolls, small candy canes, and some round lollipops with flowers painted in their centers. Each year, I decorated my tree in a different way. When I moved away from home, instead of one tree I had several small ones: one in the bedroom for the same tiny stuffed animals I'd put on my first tree; one in the kitchen with gingerbread sculpture cookies hanging from it; one in the dining room displaying birds and birds' nests; and several in the living room for my collection of folk toys and dolls from around the world. Some of the trees were made from evergreen branches tied into tree shapes with wire and string or nailed to a door or wall. Today, I make trees out of cloth and paper, too. These are easy to make and don't take up much space—and I can have as many of them as I want!

My mother and father made Christmas special for me. Every year, I waited eagerly for our family's traditional activities. We made fruitcakes together, and all cut and decorated fancy cookies. My father taught me how to cut out tissue paper snowflakes to paste on the windows when we moved out of Canada's snow into California's sunny Decembers. We told Christmas stories and sang songs, made decorations and gifts together, and finally surprised one another on Christmas morning. It was a time when we did things as a family. It didn't much matter whether the fruitcake tasted perfect, or the snowflakes looked just right—togetherness was the important thing.

This book was first planned and designed for use in the classroom, but I think it belongs in the home, too, to encourage the kind of togetherness I've been talking about. And it doesn't have to be strictly a Christmas book, either—many of the decorations and treats are just as delightful at other times of the year as they are during the Christmas season.

Basically, this book is organized according to a series of celebrations. Each chapter contains the ingredients for a month-long celebration using a historical or cultural theme, beginning with ideas for creating an appropriate environment and ending with good things to eat. Many of the crafts are rooted in myth; others, such as the crèche, stem from religion. Christmas is a worldwide celebration, and I've attempted to give the book an international flavor.

I tried to be very careful to use only the most practical materials in these projects. For years, I pored through magazines and books, looking for crafts and folk arts that I could do with children that wouldn't cost a small fortune. Some of them are simple enough that even little children can do them on their own; others require adult supervision. Before you decide to do a craft, or before encouraging a child to do it, read through it to find out what's needed and where you might have to lend a hand. I recommend that children be allowed to do as much as they can independently. That's what I see as the true meaning of learning through art.

I hope that you'll all find ideas in this book that can help to make your Christmas very special—for you, your family, your class, your friends. Christmas is a time for sharing and giving. Thank you for letting me share this Christmas with you.

Merry Christmas!

Kathryn E. Shoemaker

Table of Contents

Folk Arts for an International Christmas Celebration

This international Christmas celebration borrows folk arts and traditional decorations from Japan, Poland, Denmark, England, Africa, France, Italy, India, China, and Germany. It's a rich jumble of colors, shapes, and textures and contains the spirits of many peoples and their special ways of creating a colorful and joyous Christmas.

Room Decorations

Flags on a String (an idea from Denmark)

Materials:
- colored construction paper
- scratch paper
- scissors, glue, pencil, and ruler
- string—100' for a room decoration
  50' for a tree drape
- encyclopedia or reference book with pictures of flags from around the world
- colored felt-tipped marking pens

Look at an encyclopedia or reference book and decide which flags you want to make. Decide what the dominant color of each one is. For each flag, cut out a 6" x 5" rectangle from construction paper that's the same color as the flag's background color. Fold the piece of construction paper in half so it measures 3" x 5".

Take a piece of 3" x 5" scratch paper and draw the flag design on it. You can do this either freehand or with a ruler. Then cut out the flag's parts from the scratch paper and place them on appropriate pieces of construction paper. Try to match each color in the flag's design as closely as possible. Trace around the patterns you've cut from the scratch paper. Cut the shapes out of the colored construction paper and glue them to your background-color card to make the flag's design.

If a flag has an ornate or complicated emblem on it, squint your eyes and look at it. Then draw the basic shape you see. Cut that shape out of the color that comes closest to it, and paste the shape to your background-color card. Or draw the emblem right on the background-color card with marking pens.

Make two flag designs—one on each outer side of the folded card.

After you've glued all of the parts onto your flag card, drape the card over a string with the decorated part on the outside. Dab glue on the inside bottom edge of the folded flag and press both sides together. The card should not be glued to the string though. You should be able to slide it back and forth on the string.

Make more flags and glue each of them together along the string. Make them all different, or make a repeating pattern of several different kinds. Make as many flag strings as you want. There are twenty-four 5" flags per 10' of string.

These strings of flags can be draped around a tree, across a window, or along a wall. Or they can be hung from the ceiling.

You can make your flag strings as long or as short as you want them. If you're planning to make a lot of one kind of flag, try to cut several layers of paper at once.

Christmas Stockings from England

Cloth Stocking

Materials:
- assorted cloth scraps (Felt is ideal. However, you can use almost any kind of cloth. Tightly woven fabrics that don't fray are the most desirable. Make sure they are large enough for the stocking sizes you want to make.)
- assorted ribbon and trim scraps
- assorted buttons, beads, and other sew-ons
- needle, scissors, and thread
- newspaper and pencil
- sewing machine (optional)

Make these stockings in any shape or size. Some possible shapes are shown. For room decorations, you might want to make the stockings 15"-30" tall for visual impact.

Decide how big you want your stocking to be. Then draw a stocking that size on a sheet of newspaper. (This will be your pattern.) Draw an outline ½" around your first line. The first line you drew will be your seam line. Cut the pattern out on the outline.

Fold a piece of fabric in half, right sides together, or take two separate pieces of fabric and place their right sides together. Pin the stocking pattern onto the fabric. Cut out the stocking.

Lay the two pieces of fabric in front of you. Spread out your collection of ribbon and trim scraps. Place some of them on top of your stocking shape in various combinations. Try different combinations until you find one you like. Cut the ribbons and trims to fit the stocking.

Pin the ribbon and trim pieces you want to use onto the right side of each of the stocking cutouts. (You may wish to decorate just the front of your stocking and leave the back plain.)

Hand or machine stitch the ribbons and trims onto the stocking. Add buttons, beads, or other decorations.

Place the right sides of the two stocking shapes together. Match the edges and stitch along the sides and the foot. Don't stitch across the top. Turn your stocking right side out. Sew a loop of yarn or ribbon to the top of the stocking.

Hang your stocking from the fireplace mantle, in front of a window, or on your door.

Hello!
my name is
_____

Paper Stocking (just for looks, not for stuffing)

Materials:
- construction paper
- old magazines, Christmas cards, and Christmas wrapping paper
- scraps, fancy stickers, ribbons, and other decorative bits and pieces
- scissors, glue, and colored marking pens

These stockings can be any size you want—all the way from tiny ones to hang on a tree to giant ones to pin on a wall. You might want to make one 10' tall and work with lots of other people to decorate it. Or you might want to make one 2' high by yourself. Or you might want to make several 3" stockings and hang them on a string.

Decide how many stockings you want to make and how big you want them to be. Then draw some stocking shapes on scrap paper.

Cut out a good one and use it for a pattern. Put the pattern on a piece of construction paper. Trace around the pattern. Then cut the construction paper along the tracing line.

Look through magazines for bright patterns and colors to cut out and glue onto your stocking. Look through your collection of old Christmas cards and wrapping paper for more things to cut out and glue onto your stocking. For variety, tear out some things instead of cutting them out. The torn edges will give the stocking a different look. Arrange and rearrange your paper scraps on the stocking until you find a pattern you like. Then glue the pieces into place.

Decorate your stocking some more with ribbon scraps, fancy gold stickers, doodles made with colored marking pens, and anything else you like.

Glue a loop of yarn, ribbon, or string to the top of each stocking so you can hang it easily.

Paper Wishing Stocking

Materials:
- construction paper (12" x 18" pieces)
- plain white drawing paper
- colored marking pens or crayons
- scissors and glue
- tempera paint (optional)

Draw a large stocking shape on a piece of construction paper. Make it at least 11" high so you have lots of space to fill in.

On a piece of plain white drawing paper, draw all the things you'd like to find in your Christmas stocking this year. Color them with marking pens or crayons, or paint them. Or, make the things you'd like for Christmas out of bits of colored paper.

Cut out the things you've drawn and colored and glue them to your stocking.

Hang your stocking somewhere where your family will be sure to see it.

An International String of Stockings

Materials:
- colored construction paper
- colored marking pens
- scissors and glue
- encyclopedia, picture books, or reference books with pictures of folk designs and flags from different countries
- string

Draw a stocking on a piece of construction paper and cut it out. Then, for example, make a Mexican stocking by drawing designs from Mexican folk arts all over your stocking. Somewhere on the stocking write the name of the country and draw its flag.

Here are some sample designs you could use for stockings for the following countries: Mexico, Japan, Africa, USA, Denmark, and Russia.

Make as many stockings as you like. Glue a loop of string or yarn to the top of each stocking. Then hang them all together on a string. Hang your string of stockings in front of a window, along a wall, or anywhere you want to make bright and cheery.

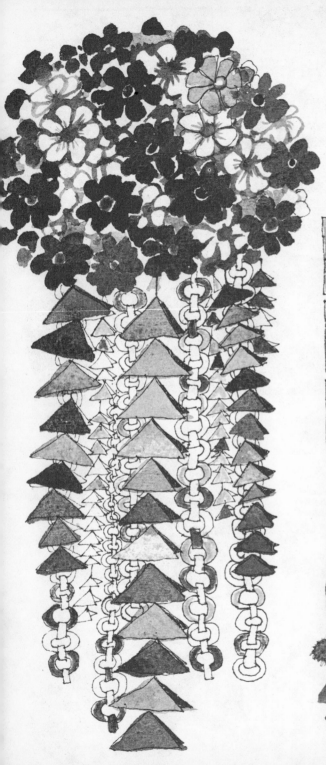

Japanese Tanabata Decoration

Materials:
- colored paper, such as origami paper or lightweight art paper
- colored tissue paper
- lightweight cardboard
- string and needle
- glue and scissors

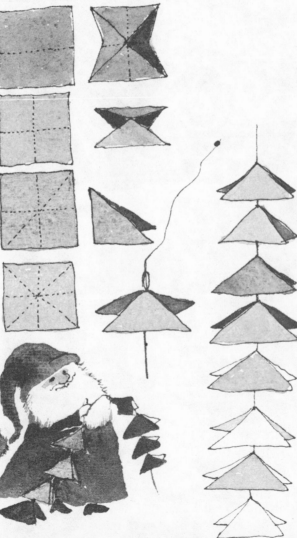

Tanabata Pyramids

Cut assorted colored papers into 5″, 6″, and 7″ squares. Fold each square in half and then fold it in half again (for quarters). Unfold the square. Turn it over and fold it on the diagonal. Unfold it and fold on the other diagonal. Push the paper gently together and up to form a pyramid.

Make as many pyramids as you want. Thread a needle with a 3′ length of string. Tie a knot at the end. Insert needle through center of pyramid and push it through the top of the pyramid. Make ten strings. Thread ten pyramids onto each string.

Tanabata Paper Chains

Cut colored paper into strips 3/4″ wide and 6″ long. Overlap the ends of one strip to form a loop, then glue the ends together. Loop the next strip through the first loop and glue the ends of the second strip together. Continue to loop new strips through closed strips until you have a paper chain that's 30″ long. Make ten strings 30″ long.

Giant Flower Balls

Cut two circles 15″ in diameter from lightweight cardboard. Cut a 5″ circle from the center of one circle and a 12″ circle from the other. Discard these two circles and keep the two rings. Make thirty 6″ tissue paper flower petals (page 27) in assorted bright colors. Glue them to the two brightly colored rings. Attach a piece of string to the ring with the 5″ hole. Hang this ring vertically from the ceiling. Attach four pieces of string 30″ long to the ring with the 12″ hole. Hang this ring horizontally from the vertical ring by tying each of the four 30″ strings through the center of the vertical ring.

Tie or glue the strings of Tanabata pyramids and paper chains so that they hang from the horizontal ring. Hang the whole thing from the ceiling indoors or from a tree or pole outdoors.

Santa Claus Around the World
(a string of paper dolls to hang around a room)

Almost every country has a Christmas gift-giver—Santa Claus, Father Christmas, Lady Befana, Sinterklaas, Tomten, Nisse, or Gnomes.

Basic Paper Doll

Materials:
- construction paper (large pieces)
- scissors
- marking pens or paints
- clear cellophane tape
- encyclopedia, reference book, or picture book showing costumes of different countries

Decide how large you want each doll to be (6″, 9″, 12″, or 15″). Then take two or more sheets of construction paper and tape them together, end to end, with clear cellophane tape.

Fold the paper into several parallel sections. Each section should be the same size and should be wide enough so you can draw a doll on it. When you're done folding, the paper should look like an accordion.

Then, with the paper accordion-pleated, lightly sketch a figure on the top panel. Draw the figure so that each of its hands stretches out and touches a fold.

Cut around the doll, cutting through all the paper layers at the same time. Be careful not to cut through the fold where the hands meet, or you'll end up with separate dolls instead of a string of them. When you're finished cutting, unfold carefully.

Paint or color the front side of each figure in the chain.

For variety, fold another piece of paper and draw a different figure on each panel. Make sure that the figures on joining panels hold hands. You might want to make one of the figures a child and the other a Christmas gift-giver, such as Santa Claus. Paint international costumes on the figures. If, for example, you draw a child in a Norwegian costume, then draw a Norwegian costume on the Santa he or she is holding hands with. Then you might want to draw an Eskimo child and an Eskimo Santa, and so on. You also might want to look at a reference book to find out about the gift-givers in different countries. Not every country has a Santa Claus dressed in red velvet and white fur. When you're finished with your paper-doll chain, hang it in front of a window or along a wall.

Santa and Two Children
(large cardboard paper dolls)

These dolls can be used to show the Christmas folk costumes from many lands. The two children dolls can also be used to show the costumes for other celebrations during the year. Make as many costumes for the dolls as you like.

Basic Paper Dolls

Materials:
- lightweight cardboard
- pencil, scissors, and glue
- colored marking pens
- heavy drawing paper in skin tones
- yarn scraps—red, brown, black, yellow, white (hair colors)
- scratch paper

On scratch paper, draw a 10″ high adult figure and two 7″ high children with extended arms and legs. When your figures look the way you want them to, cut them out. Place your figures on a piece of heavy drawing paper. Trace around them. Cut them out of the drawing paper, and glue each of them to a piece of lightweight cardboard. Cut them out again.

Draw faces on your dolls with colored marking pens.

Make hair for your paper dolls out of yarn scraps. For long hair, tie a bundle of yarn scraps together in the middle. Glue this bundle to the doll's head. For short hair, cut shorter pieces of yarn and glue each piece individually to the doll's head.

Costumes for Paper Dolls

Materials:
- paper scraps
- plain white drawing paper or lightweight construction paper
- scissors and glue
- encyclopedia, reference book, or picture book showing folk costumes from many lands
- colored pencils and marking pens
- fabric scraps, rickrack, buttons, beads, and other decorative glue-ons (optional)

Look at an encyclopedia or reference book and decide which folk costumes you want to make. Then place one of your prepared paper dolls on a piece of white paper. Very lightly trace around the doll with a pencil to make a pattern. This pattern shows you how big a piece of clothing for the doll needs to be. Draw a piece of clothing on the pattern. Then draw tabs on the piece of clothing at the shoulders. Color the piece of clothing and cut it out.

Instead of coloring the clothes, try gluing pieces of cloth onto them. You could also glue pieces of rickrack, ribbon, buttons, beads, or whatever else you like onto the clothes.

Make several costumes for each doll.

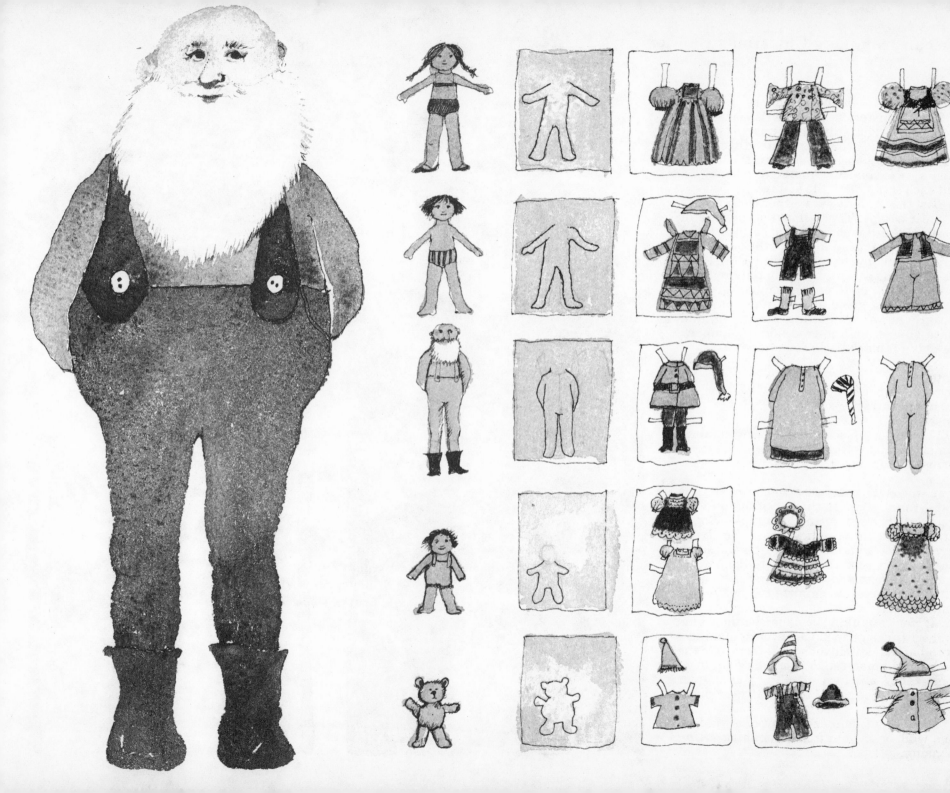

African Dahomey Christmas Banner

The original Dahomey banners made in Africa are historical documents sewn from cloth scraps. The banners are passed on from one generation to the next. Instead of cutting the cloth into specific shapes, the artists often work exclusively from scraps, believing that each scrap has a life of its own.

Try this project with either cloth scraps or paper scraps. Try to imagine the kind of shapes the scraps suggest, and build on those shapes and suggestions. Give the banners a holiday look by trying to find Christmas shapes in the scraps; by using only red and white paper or cloth on a green background; by looking for green shapes to put on a red background; or by putting red, green, and white shapes on the traditional Dahomey dark blue or black background.

Materials:
- cloth or paper scraps
- scissors and glue
- needle, pins, and thread
- 15″ x 30″ long piece of tightly woven fabric in chosen background color or big piece of construction paper

Look through your assortment of scraps and arrange some on the background fabric or paper. Play with them. Put scraps on top of scraps to create specific shapes. See what tiny cutouts can do for your pattern. A scrap may suggest something to you. Sometimes you will have to add more scraps or even cut out extra pieces to complete the image you want to make.

If you're making a paper banner, glue your scrap design in place. If you're making a cloth banner, stitch your fabric scraps to the background material. You might want to do some fancy stitchery to give your banner more detail. See page 110 for stitchery directions.

Hang your banner in front of a window, on a wall, or on your front door as a greeting to visitors.

Advent Calendar (a German tradition)

To mark each day of the month before Christmas, make an Advent Calendar that indicates what kinds of things people in other countries are celebrating during December.

Materials:
- construction paper
- large piece of cardboard (28″ x 28″), string (at least 120″), or long scroll of paper (120″ x 6″)
- scissors and glue
- pins
- colored marking pens
- encyclopedia, reference book, or picture book showing Christmas celebrations in many different countries

Make twenty-four 4″ x 8″ cards out of construction paper and fold each of them in half lengthwise, thus making a 4″ x 4″ square. On the outside of each card, print a number from 1 to 24. Inside each card, write the name of a country and a little bit about the country's Christmas celebrations and customs. Around each number, draw and color a folk toy or doll representing the country mentioned inside. There'll be a card for each day of the month until Christmas.

Glue the cards in traditional calendar style on a large piece of cardboard; or pin them to a long string and drape them across a window; or pin them to a long scroll of paper and pin the scroll to a wall.

Danish Christmas Seals

A Danish tradition that's become international is the annual designing of a Christmas seal. The first Christmas seal was designed in 1904.

Make your own seal to use on Christmas letters, cards, and presents. When someone uses Christmas seals, it means that he or she has given money or time to a charitable cause. Your own Christmas seal could represent something you care about, such as saving some endangered animal species. Or, your seal could be the symbol of a particular charity or cause.

Christmas Seal Stamp

Materials:
- large rubber eraser, art foam, or a small linoleum block
- a stamp pad or linoleum ink
- X-acto knife
- scratch paper and pencil

Sketch a design for your Christmas seal on scratch paper. Remember that a stamp design has to be drawn on backwards. If you use words, remember to write them in mirror image. (Write or print the words, and then hold them up to a mirror to see how they look.)

Draw the design onto the eraser or linoleum block. Gently cut away the areas around and inside your design—the areas which you don't want to print when you use your stamp. The design area should stand out about ⅛″ from the rest of the eraser or linoleum block.

Ink your Christmas seal stamp. Then practice using it. If you've made your stamp out of an eraser, be sure to press down gently to get a clear impression of your design.

Stick-on Christmas Seals

Materials:
- white drawing paper or typing paper (8½″ x 11″)
- pen with black ink
- colored marking pens
- Lepages glue
- water
- scissors

Draw several Christmas seal designs on a white sheet of paper with a pen that has black ink in it. Then make as many photocopies of your design as you need. (For example, if you draw twenty designs and then make five photocopies, you'll have one hundred Christmas seals.)

Use marking pens to color each Christmas seal design. Then paint the back of each sheet of paper with a mixture of Lepages glue and water in equal amounts.

Let the sheet of seal designs dry thoroughly, glue side up. When the sheets are dry, cut the stamps out. When you're ready to use one, lick its back and stick it to your letter or package.

The Crèche

In southern France, crafts people make small, colorful clay figures to sell at Christmastime. These people are known as santon makers, or santonniers, because, in addition to making figures representing Mary, Joseph, the infant Jesus, and the shepherds, these artisans also make little saints (or *santons*) to place around the crèche. The santons represent local people as well as traditional saints. Traditionally, the figures are placed on a bed of sprouted lentils or grass seed. Holly, rosemary, and other herbs are also placed around the nativity scene.

Materials:
- terra cotta or commercial clay substitute
- clear plastic or acrylic spray
- texturing tools such as seed pods, kitchen utensils, toothpicks, and fabrics with raised patterns
- wood board to roll clay on
- tempera or acrylic paints and brushes
- kitchen knife

Begin this project by softening the clay in your hands. As you soften the clay, think about the extra characters or little santons you will want to add to your nativity scene. Perhaps you could make some school friends, family members, or favorite pets.

To make your first figure, roll some clay into a 1½″ thick coil. Then roll a lump of clay into a ball and flatten it on one side. This will be the base for your figure.

Stick the clay coil onto the clay base. Roll some thin coils to use as arms. Roll a small ball to use as a head. Carefully join the head to the figure, working clay from the coil and the ball together.

Make facial features with a toothpick or clay tool. Add small amounts of moistened clay to create hair and headgear.

If you make a full-skirted figure, such as Mary, Joseph, or one of the shepherds or wise men, hollow out the figure by scooping out the clay inside the skirt with a spoon. Work through the bottom of the base.

Make as many figures as you want for your crèche scene.

If you used terra cotta, let the figures dry thoroughly and, if possible, fire them in a kiln. If you used a clay substitute, dry according to the accompanying instructions.

After the figures have dried, paint them with tempera or acrylic paints and then spray or paint them with a clear plastic finish.

In keeping with the international spirit of this celebration, make the characters around your crèche represent people from different countries.

An International Collection of Christmas Tree Ornaments

Italian Nutshell Babies

Materials:
- empty walnut shells
- small scraps of fabric, lace, and yarn
- cotton batik or polyester stuffing
- tiny beads or buttons for eyes
- scissors and glue
- thread (about the same color as a nylon stocking)
- fancy thread (Gold is extra nice.)
- an old nylon stocking
- red or pink permanent marking pen

Carefully crack some walnuts so that the half shells are intact.

Cut a 2″ circle out of a nylon stocking. Take a 1″ ball of cotton or polyester stuffing and pull the 2″ circle of nylon around it. Tie the circle shut with thread. This ball will be the head of your nutshell baby.

Glue a few pieces of yarn to the head for hair. Glue a little piece of lace around the head to make a cap.

Thread a needle with thread which is the same color as the nylon stocking. Sew two tiny beads or buttons to the head to make eyes. Use a permanent marking pen to make rosy cheeks. (A water-based pen will run.)

Press some cotton into the nutshell. Glue a piece of fabric over the cotton. Place the tiny, bonneted baby head at one end of the shell. Glue it down. Cut a small piece of fabric for a blanket. Tuck the fabric into the shell like a blanket leaving only the baby's head exposed. Dab glue between the fabric and the sides of the shell.

Thread a needle with an 8″ piece of gold thread. Do not tie a knot in it. Insert the needle at the edge of the blanket on one side of the shell and come out on the opposite side. Remove the needle. Tie the ends together so that you can hang the nutshell cradle from the Christmas tree.

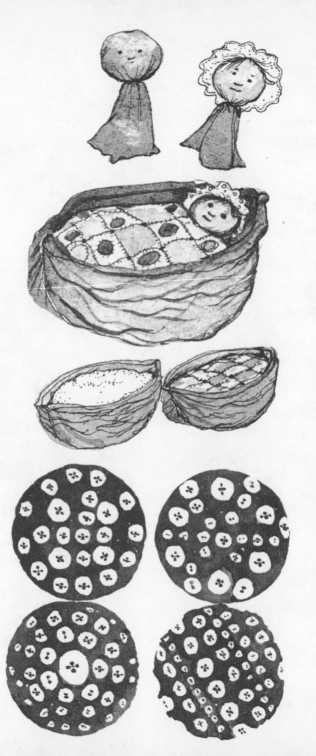

English Pearlies

Materials:
- cloth scraps (Felt is ideal.)
- lightweight cardboard
- scissors, needle, and thread
- buttons (all kinds and sizes—The Salvation Army thrift stores sell bags of buttons very cheaply.)
- cotton, polyester stuffing, or old nylon stocking scraps
- small amount of yarn or thread

Flat Pearlies

To make each ornament, cut two 4″ circles of cloth and one 4″ circle of cardboard. Place buttons on the two cloth circles in decorative arrangements, and stitch them into place after you've created a pleasing design.

Glue a 4″ decorated cloth circle to each side of the 4″ cardboard circle.

Attach a yarn or thread loop to your pearlie for easy hanging.

Three-dimensional Pearlies

To make a three-dimensional pearlie ball, cut two 4″ circles out of cloth. Stitch right sides together leaving a 1″ opening. Turn the piece right side out.

Stuff your pearlie ball with cotton, polyester stuffing, or scraps of nylon stockings. Then, stitch up the 1″ opening.

Sew on as many buttons as you like. Then attach a yarn or thread loop to your three-dimensional pearlie for easy hanging.

Japanese Thread Balls

Materials:
- 3″ styrofoam balls, old plastic balls, or wads of newspaper taped into ball shapes (These will take a little time and effort to make, but they're cheaper than styrofoam.)
- glue
- ribbon scraps of various colors, colored yarns, or embroidery thread

For each ornament, brush a little glue onto the ball to hold the first piece of yarn, ribbon, or thread in place. (Or, hold the yarn, ribbon, or thread against the ball with the thumb of one hand while using the other hand to wind with.) Start wrapping ribbon, yarn, or thread around the ball six to ten times in one direction, then six to ten times in another direction. Continue to change winding directions. Change colors as often as you like, tying new colors onto old ones. Change the width of the ribbon, yarn, or thread as well as the color to vary the design. Continue wrapping the ball until it's as thick and colorful as you want. Then glue the last end of the yarn, ribbon, or thread under a wrapped piece to finish the ball. Tie a loop of yarn or thread to the finished ornament so you can hang it easily.

Stuffed Dolls and Animals from India

Materials:
- cloth scraps (10″ x 8″ if possible)
- embroidery thread
- cotton, polyester stuffing, or old nylon stocking scraps
- pins, needles, thread, and scissors
- glue
- small mirrors from a craft shop or pieces of aluminum TV dinner or pie pans cut into ¼″ squares and circles
- scratch paper and pencil

Practice drawing dolls and animals on scratch paper. Make them between 5″ and 8″ high. When you've made one you like, cut it out for a pattern.

Fold a cloth scrap in half. Pin the pattern onto the cloth and cut. You will have two animals.

Stitch right sides together along the edges, leaving a 2″ opening. Turn the piece right side out. Stuff the doll or animal.

Begin to place cloth scraps and tiny mirrors on the stuffed animal or doll. When you like an arrangement, sew it in place. Glue the mirrors onto the doll or animal. Add a thread loop to the ornament for easy hanging.

English Crackers

Materials:
- empty toilet paper rolls or other lightweight cardboard tubes
- crepe paper
- bits of gold foil
- tissue paper
- scissors and glue
- gold thread

Real English party crackers pop, but the ones you'll be making will just be decorative. They can be opened to reveal a tissue-paper party hat with a tiny gift, Christmas greeting, or fortune tucked inside.

Cut the cardboard tubing into 2"-3" lengths.

Make paper hats. For each hat, cut two pieces of tissue paper the same shape. Glue the pieces together along the side.

Cut decorative, colored shapes from tissue paper and/or gold foil. Glue these shapes onto the hat.

When the hat is thoroughly dried, fold it as small as possible and place it inside a piece of tubing.

You may also want to put a small gift inside the tubing. Or, put a small piece of paper with a Christmas greeting or a fortune printed on it inside each tube.

Out of colored crepe paper cut an 8" square. Gently fold into 1" accordion folds.

Cut each end of your folded crepe paper into fringes or scallops.

Unfold and wrap the crepe paper around the tube so that 3" of paper extend beyond each end of the tube. Twist the paper together at each end.

Cut a gold seal or fancy shape to glue where the crepe paper overlaps.

Tie each cracker onto the tree with a thin piece of gold thread. Or follow the English tradition and place several crackers on a party table. Use them as place cards by gluing a small piece of paper to the middle of each one.

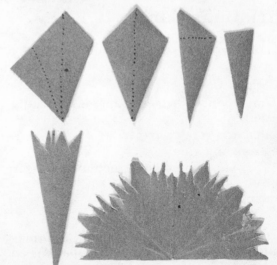

The Polish Riband

Materials:
- colored construction paper
- scissors and glue
- yarn or thread for loop

Fold a 4″ square of paper as shown. Unfold it. This is your 4″ medallion.

Cut small medallions, flowers, or figures out of colored construction paper. Glue these onto the large medallion.

To make two decorative streamers to add to the medallion, fold two pieces of 8″ x 2″ paper in half lengthwise. Then cut designs along the unfolded edges. Cut successively smaller streamers to glue onto the two main streamers. Glue the completed streamers to the large medallion.

Add a yarn or thread loop to the ornament for easy hanging.

Christmas Cards

Polish Wycinanki (paper cutouts)

Materials:

- colored paper (Origami paper is especially good.)
- pencil and scratch paper
- scissors and glue
- 8½″ x 11″ colored construction paper for cards
- tracing paper

Sketch some bouquets or simple Christmas figures on a piece of scratch paper. When you've made a picture you like, cut it out to use as a pattern.

Choose a piece of 8½″ x 11″ colored construction paper and fold it in half to make a Christmas card. Place your pattern on the front side of the card and trace around it. Cut out the traced picture. Discard the cutout piece. You now have a window on page one of your card.

Trace your pattern on a piece of paper of a different color from your card. Cut out the traced picture and glue this piece to the inside of your card. Through the window on the front side of the card you can now see the piece glued onto page three.

Select another color to work with. Cut out pieces of this colored paper to add detail to the cutout you glued to the inside of your card. (For example, if your original cutout was a green Christmas tree, you may want to cut out colored-paper ornaments to glue on the tree.) Continue to cut and glue small pieces of paper onto the page three cutout to fill in all the details of your original sketch.

Glue some small cutouts to the front of your card around the window.

Chinese Straw Mosaic Cards

Materials:
- real straw (available at feed stores)
- an iron
- sharp knife
- glue and scissors
- finely pointed felt-tipped marking pens in assorted bright colors
- 8½″ x 11″ construction paper or heavy drawing paper (one piece for each card)
- tracing paper or lightweight typing paper

Slit straws with a sharp knife. Soak straws in warm water for two hours. Shake off water, and iron each straw flat.

Fold a piece of construction paper or heavy drawing paper in half to make a Christmas card. On the front side, draw a Christmas picture or design. (The shapes in your picture or design should be quite large.)

Trace your picture or design onto a piece of tracing paper or lightweight typing paper. Or, trace each section of your picture or design on a separate sheet of paper.

Glue pieces of straw side-by-side onto your traced picture or design until you've covered it. Iron flat, and let dry completely.

After the glue has dried, color each section of your picture or design a different color with felt-tipped marking pens. Glue each section down where it belongs on your Christmas card. Let dry thoroughly.

If you can't find any straw, use tiny strips of colored paper instead. (You won't have to soak them or iron them, of course.)

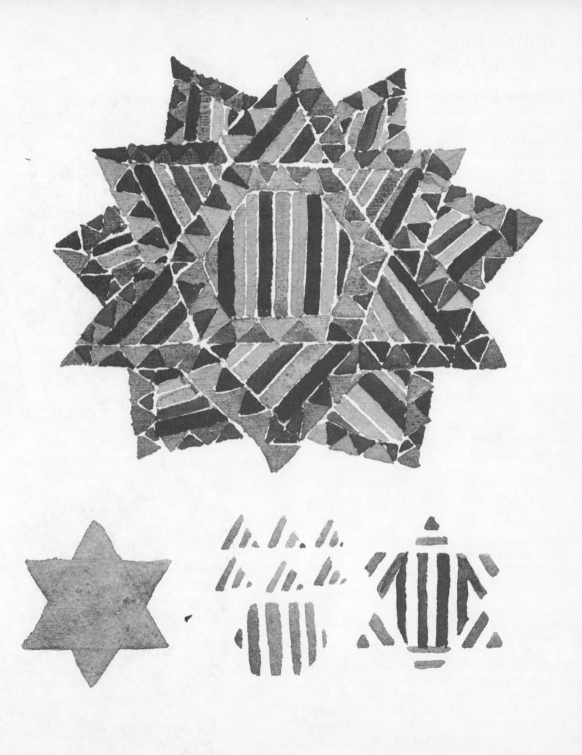

Wrapping Papers From Japan and Africa

Japanese Dip-and-Dye Paper

Materials:
- newspaper
- tissue paper or rice paper
- food coloring
- bowls for dyes
- water
- an iron

Spread newspaper over your work area.

Fold a piece of tissue or rice paper as shown:

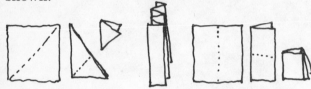

Pour 1 cup water into each bowl. Add food coloring. Dip the corners of the folded paper into dye. Carefully unfold paper. Place on newspapers to dry.

When paper is completely dry, iron out creases.

African Doodle Paper

Materials:
- tissue paper
- colored marking pens
- scratch paper for practice
- an iron

Practice drawing a small doodle on a piece of scratch paper.

Fold the tissue paper into sections. Then fold into more sections. Draw along the fold lines with colored marking pens. Start filling in each section with repeated doodles. Use Christmas colors, Christmas figures, or both.

After you have filled each folded section with a doodle, iron out the creases in your wrapping paper.

African Adinkira Stamping

Materials:
- tissue paper
- art foam or thin sponge sheets sold by the roll
- stamp pads and stamp pad inks—red, green, black
- colored marking pens
- scissors and glue
- cardboard
- an iron

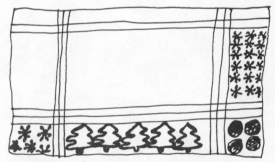

Make up some designs and try them out on scratch paper. When you find some you like, cut them out to use as patterns.

Place your patterns on art foam or sponge sheets and trace around them. Cut them out and glue each one to a separate piece of cardboard to make stamps. (Be careful not to let the glue soak all the way through the foam or sponge because it will clog your stamp.)

Fold tissue paper into sections. Draw along the fold lines with colored marking pens. Stamp a design into each section of the paper.

After you have stamped each section, iron out the creases in your wrapping paper.

23

A Latin American Christmas Celebration

A rustle of brightly colored tissue paper, a room full of flowers. A feeling of clay. Figures and animals—painted, drawn, and molded onto and out of clay and other materials. Bright colors, bright sounds, dancing, and festive foods. That's what this celebration can be. A Latin American Christmas celebration is a warm and sunny one.

Room Decorations

Paper Banners

Materials:
- colored tissue paper
- sharp scissors (Nail scissors are ideal.)
- colored string
- glue

Cut tissue paper into large squares or rectangles (any size you like).

Accordion pleat a piece of square or rectangular tissue paper into parallel folds of four, six, or eight sections.

Cut away pieces of paper from the folded sides. Cut as much and as many pieces away as you like, but do not completely cut from one fold to the opposite fold because that will cut the banner into separate pieces.

Carefully unfold the cut tissue paper. (This is your cutout banner.) Then glue your banner to a piece of string. Make more banners to glue onto the string.

Hang your banners on the wall or in a window.

Paper Flowers

These can be made in any size. Several flowers 5"-7" in diameter can quickly brighten a room.

Materials:
- colored tissue paper or colored crepe paper
- scissors, string, and glue
- masking tape or green florist's tape
- thin wire

Accordion pleat a piece of colored tissue or crepe paper into parallel sections of desired width. Hold the accordion-pleated paper carefully. Then scallop the right-hand folds (or the left-hand if you are left handed). Cut off the left-hand fold. Gather the straight edges, turning the flower as each new length is added and gathered. Push and pull tissue into a pleasing shape. Wind and tie string or wire around the gathered base.

Or fringe both edges of a section of tissue. Unfold the tissue and gather through the center. For multicolored flowers, alternate the colors before gathering. Tie with wire or string.

Or cut petal shapes out of tissue paper. Make rounded or pointed petals. Gather and tie at the bottom.

27

Piñatas

Piñatas can be made in any size or shape. They can be filled with candies, nuts, and small treats or just used as decorations. Originally, piñatas were made of clay pots. Today, most are made with cardboard candy containers.

Materials:
- newspaper
- paper bags
- masking tape and stapler
- white glue and string
- flour and water mixed to the consistency of pancake batter (or liquid starch)
- colored tissue paper

Decide on what piñata figure you want to make—doll; animal figure, such as a donkey; or an inanimate figure, such as a star.

Basic Piñata Shape

To make the basic shape, stuff a large paper bag with newspapers crushed into balls. Tie or tape the top of the bag shut.

To make a head for the piñata, stuff a smaller bag with newspapers. Tie the smaller bag over the tied end of the large bag.

To add arms, legs, ears, tails, star points, etc., fold or roll newspapers into desired thicknesses and lengths. Cut ears out of several layers of paper. Staple or tape these rough shapes onto the basic paper-bag construction.

Mix flour and water to a consistency like pancake batter. (Or use liquid starch instead.) Tear newspapers into 1″ wide strips. Dip each strip into the flour and water mixture and press the strip around the stuffed paper bags. If you want to stuff your piñata with treats, leave one 3″ in diameter spot free of wet newspaper strips. Secure arms, legs, or other additions with strips of newspaper soaked in flour and water or starch. Add several wet strips at the juncture of the stuffed paper bags and the arms or legs until additions feel secure.

Smooth the piñata shape as you work. Be sure to press down the edges of the newspaper strips.

Keep adding newspaper strips until you've covered the basic bag construction with three layers of newspaper strips dipped

in flour and water or starch. Then let your piñata dry thoroughly for one to three days.

While the basic shape is drying, prepare the tissue-paper curls. (See page 30.)

When the basic piñata shape is dry, cut open a 3″ door in the spot you kept free of wet newspaper strips. Pull out the crushed newspaper within the piñata.

Begin to glue tissue-paper curls from the bottom up. Glue each tissue-paper strip over the straight edge of the previously glued strip. Tiny dots of white glue are sufficient to hold tissue in place. Glue curls onto the 3″ door.

Stuff the hollow piñata with treats. Tape the door shut. Tie a heavy string around the piñata's neck or body, whichever balances best.

Cut layers of tissue paper into long strips. Each strip should be 4″ wide and the length of the tissue paper.

Fold the strips lengthwise so that you have several 2″ wide strips.

Fold each strip several times. The number of layers you fold depends upon how many layers your scissors can cut at one time.

Along the folded edge of each 2″ wide strip, cut a fringe by cutting 1½″ down into the tissue strip at ¼″ intervals. When you've cut a fringe along the entire folded edge of a tissue-paper strip, open the strip to its 4″ height again.

Dot glue along one edge of the strip. A little bit of glue is all you need. Then fold the other edge of the tissue back onto the edge with glue. (Fold the paper in the opposite direction of the first fold you made to cut the fringe.) Press shut. The tissue-paper strip now forms a rounded curl.

These strips of curls can be made in different sizes. For example, the ears of the piñata figure might require finished curls only 1″ high while a tail or horse's mane might need curls 4″ high.

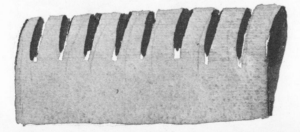

Piñata Trees

You can make a free-standing Christmas tree with tissue paper cut, folded, and glued into piñata curls.

Materials:
- green tissue paper
- large cardboard sheet taped into a cone shape of the desired size or wadded up newspapers taped and tied into a large cone shape
- glue

Make a cone out of cardboard or newspaper.

Cut, fold, and glue green tissue paper into piñata curls.

Glue the green curls to the cone, starting at the bottom and working up. Tiny dots of glue are all you will need.

Advent Calendar

With the room brightly decorated, you can begin the month-long Christmas celebration by making a large Advent Calendar on the wall.

Here's one suggestion for an Advent Calendar using a variation of Mexican bark painting.

Materials:
- butcher paper or brown construction paper
- pencil
- scraps of colored construction paper
- tempera paints and brushes
- fine point black marking pens
- an iron

Cut two pieces of paper 20" x 40". (This is only a suggested size.) If you use butcher paper, paint them with brown tempera. Crumple them. Dry them. Iron them flat. This procedure leaves the paper looking like weathered bark.

On a piece of scratch paper, sketch a picture of twenty-four birds, flowers, and butterflies on a background of trees and lush plants. Paint the trees and plants from your design on one piece of dried butcher paper.

Draw the twenty-four items in your picture on the second piece of butcher paper. Cut out each item. Fill in the details of each of your twenty-four cutouts with tempera.

With a black, fine point marking pen, go over your picture and the twenty-four items. Draw decorative details and outline everything. Write a number from 1 to 24 on each of the items.

Write a thought-provoking phrase or quotation on the back of each of the twenty-four cutouts. Pin up the cutouts day by day or put them all up at the beginning of Advent. Read one of them on each day of Advent.

Paper Tree of Life

The green Christmas tree that we know is one version of the Tree of Life that has come to be associated with Christmas. In the spirit of a Latin American Christmas, make a large paper Tree of Life using the traditional Mexican candleholder as a design.

Materials:
- scratch paper and pencil
- scissors, glue, and pins
- colored construction paper and assorted paper scraps
- reference book, encyclopedia, or picture book showing what a Mexican Tree of Life looks like
- lightweight cardboard or heavy paper
- tempera paint and brushes
- background material, such as a large piece of cardboard or colored butcher paper

On scratch paper, sketch possible shapes for your Tree of Life.

Also sketch some of the items you want to decorate your tree with, like flowers, animals, people, or shapes. You might choose a theme for your Tree of Life, such as favorite story characters, Christmas symbols, baby animals, flowers, things that begin with "B," or something for every letter of the alphabet.

The basic shape may be painted onto a background with tempera paints. It can also be made with cut or torn pieces of paper glued or pinned to the background.

Decorate the basic shape with flowery designs. Paint them on, or make them out of more cut or torn paper.

Make the items that you want to hang from your Tree of Life. Sketch them onto lightweight cardboard or heavy paper. Paint them or fill them in with pieces of cut or torn colored paper.

Pin all the items to the Tree of Life. The items will also make lovely decorations for a traditional Christmas tree next year or later in the Christmas season.

If you've been busy making paper banners, paper flowers, piñatas, a piñata tree, and a large Tree of Life, you have almost all

the ingredients you need for a truly festive Latin American Christmas room. Hang the banners and flowers from the ceiling. Hang them in windows. Hang up the piñata (or piñatas, if you made several). Colored crepe paper streamers can add to the room's decorations. If you've made a free–standing piñata tree, you may also want to make some of the ornaments found on pages 38-43.

The Crèche

Another important part of a Latin American Christmas celebration is the crèche. Here are three ways to make one.

Small Clay-Figures Crèche

Materials:
- clay or oven-hardened clays available at most art supply stores
- tempera paints and brushes
- wood board to work on
- a small dish of water

These figures can all be made by pushing and pulling small lumps of clay into figures 2" to 3" high. Push your thumb into a lump of clay to start a small pinch pot. Add a small lump of clay to the bottom of the pot by using a small amount of water like glue. Work the two pieces together. Pull the addition up into a neck and head shape. Roll a small piece of clay into a coil to use for arms. Add arm shapes to body with a bit more water. Work them into the torso until there is no visible connection mark on the clay. Roll out tiny coils to create hair and facial features and add decorative detail to the figure.

Depending upon the clay used, fire in a kiln or dry in an oven according to directions on the clay substitute package.

Paint the figures and embellish them with decorative flowers and designs such as the ones shown on this page.

Variation:
Make a crèche out of papier-mâché. Follow the directions on page 112.

Repeat the procedure until you've made all the figures and animals you want for your crèche.

Paint the figures with tempera. Dry. Arrange them on a bed of shredded construction paper.

Ecuadorian Bread-Dough Crèche

Materials:
- small shoebox
- cheap white bread
- white glue
- cold cream
- tempera or acrylic paints to color the dough
- garlic press
- toothpicks for doing detail work

Remove the crusts from twenty-four slices of white bread. Crumble bread into a bowl and add 12 oz. of white glue. Rub cold cream on your hands and then mix glue and bread together with your hands. Knead the mixture until it's no longer sticky. Divide the mixture evenly into two balls. Divide one of the balls into as many balls as you want colors for details (five to ten). Knead a different dab of paint color into each of the balls. Use the uncolored ball of dough to make the basic crèche figures. This recipe makes about seven 3″ figures.

Mix water and white glue in equal parts. Brush this mixture onto one of the crèche figures. With rolls, coils, and tiny balls of the colored dough, add details such as hair, eyes, skirts, blouses, flowers on dresses, and belts to the basic figure. Press the added details onto the figure and then brush the entire finished figure with the water-glue mixture. Make as many figures as you want for your crèche.

Paint the small box with tempera. Let dry.

Decorate the small box with designs made from the colored dough. Glue them onto the box with white glue. Make a bed of hay out of yellow dough squeezed through a garlic press. Glue the crèche figures into the box.

Latin American Folk Art Ornaments

These techniques can be used to make ornaments for piñata trees or for a traditional Christmas tree. These ornaments can also be used as parts of a Christmas mobile or for an Advent Calendar.

Ecuadorian Bread-Dough Figures

Follow the directions on page 36. Then add loops of thread for easy hanging.

Tin Ornaments

Materials:
- heavy foil or lightweight aluminum pie and TV dinner trays
- scissors and thread
- colored marking pens (permanent ink)
- scratch paper and pencil

Sketch simple shapes on scratch paper and cut them out. Place shapes on foil or aluminum and trace around them with a black marking pen. Cut the shapes out of the foil or aluminum and color them with marking pens. Punch a small hole in the top of each ornament and slip a piece of thread through the hole for easy hanging.

Alternate method:

Materials:
- tin can tops
- sandpaper
- colored marking pens (permanent ink)
- yarn
- hole punch

Save assorted tin can tops. Sand away rough edges. Draw and color designs on them with permanent marking pens.
   Punch a small hole in the top of each ornament. Thread with yarn for hanging.

Piñata Balls

Materials:
- colored tissue paper
- newspapers
- masking tape, white glue, and scissors
- thread

Follow the directions on page 30 for making piñata curls. Make an assortment of curls ½" to 1" high in a variety of colors.

Crush a sheet of newspaper into a tight ball. Wrap a few strips of masking tape around it. Glue piñata curls all around the ball. Add a loop of thread to your ornament for easy hanging.

Mini-Piñatas

Materials:
- colored tissue paper
- styrofoam cups
- white glue and scissors
- thread

Make 1" piñata curls. (See page 30.)

Tape two styrofoam cups together. Glue piñata curls all around the cups. Add a loop of thread to your ornament for easy hanging.

Small Piñata Figures

Materials:
- newspapers
- colored tissue paper
- colored construction paper
- glue, scissors, masking tape, and thread

For each figure, crush newspaper into a tight 5" ball. Secure with masking tape. Make a head out of a small wad of newspaper and tape it to the first ball. Cut arms, legs, ears, and whatever else you need out of construction paper and tape them to the newspaper figure.

Follow the directions on page 30 for making piñata curls. Make an assortment of curls 1" high in a variety of colors. Then glue the piñata curls all over the figure. Add a loop of thread for easy hanging.

Tiny Clay Suns

Materials:
- terra cotta or clay substitute
- nichrome wire (green florist's wire at floral supply shop)
- texturing tools such as forks, spoons, seed pods, twigs, nuts, bolts, buttons—anything that will make an interesting pattern when pressed into the clay
- tempera or acrylic paints

Make two small pinch pots 1"-2" in diameter.

Put a small wad of newspaper between them as a filler. Squeeze the outside edges of the two pots together. Work the edges together until you can't see where they're joined. If there's enough clay, pull out small points from the ball's surface to make your sun's rays. Or you can work small dabs of clay onto the ball and pull them into points.

Texture the sun with any or all of the texture tools you've gathered. Add features such as eyes, nose, and mouth with small bits or coils of clay.

Insert a loop of nichrome wire into one edge of the sun.

Dry, fire, or bake your clay sun according to the specific directions given with your clay.

After your sun has been dried, fired, or baked, decorate it with tempera or acrylic paints. Add flowers and curlicues.

Papier-Maché Doll or Puppet
(5"-7" tall)

Follow the basic instructions on page 112 for making the basic doll.

Paint your doll with decorative details in a variety of colors. If you have some, you may want to use yarn scraps and cloth scraps for hair and clothing.

If you want to make your doll into a string puppet, insert small wire loops into hammered holes in each hand, each foot, and through the top of the doll's head. Tie string to each loop. Attach the other ends of the strings to a wooden strip.

More Latin American Christmas Tree Ornaments

Make some tiny molas out of felt or colored construction paper according to the directions on page 44.

Paper flowers like the ones on page 27 can also be made on a much smaller scale. They could be hung separately, gathered into small bouquets, or strung into long garlands to drape around the Christmas tree.

You can also do bark paintings on 2"-3" circles of brown cardboard. (See page 31.)

Clay and Yarn Ornaments

Materials:
- terra cotta
- nichrome wire (green florist's wire)
- colored yarn scraps
- glue and scissors

Make small simple clay figures and animals, following the directions on page 35. While clay is wet, insert a small loop of nichrome wire in the top middle section of the figure. Allow clay items to dry thoroughly, and then fire them in a kiln, if possible. Cover dried or fired items with colored yarn following the directions on page 47.

Yarn Pompon

Materials:
- yarn
- cardboard
- scissors and yarn needle

Cut two cardboard circles as big around as you want your pompon to be. Then cut a ¼″ hole in the center of each circle.

Thread a yarn needle with two long strands of yarn. Place the cardboard circles together so that the holes match up. Then push the needle up through the holes in the circles and pull the yarn through. (Hold the end of the yarn under the circles with two fingers of the hand that isn't holding the needle.) Bring the needle around and through the bottom of the circles again. Keep bringing the yarn through the hole and wrapping it around the circles until you've covered both circles with yarn. Don't pull the yarn too tight, though. If you want an especially fluffy pompon, cover the circles with several layers of yarn. If you run out of yarn on your needle, simple cut the strands off close to the needle and rethread the needle—you can trim the rough edges later.

When you have as much yarn on your circles as you want, slip a scissors between the two cardboard circles and cut all the yarn strands at the outside edge.

Insert a strand of yarn between the two circles and wind it tightly around all the lengths of yarn inside several times. Then knot the strand, leaving long ends so you can attach your pompon to something later. Remove the two cardboard circles, and fluff out the pompon.

Yarn Tassel

Materials:
- yarn
- cardboard
- scissors

Decide how long you want your tassel to be, and cut a piece of cardboard that long and about 2″ wide. Wind yarn around the length of the cardboard twenty times or more, depending on how thick the yarn is and how plump you want your tassel to be. Then tie the yarn strands together tightly at one end of the cardboard, as shown, leaving at least 3″ ends on the ties. At the other end of the cardboard, slip a scissors in between the cardboard and the yarn; clip all the yarn strands.

Tightly wrap a piece of yarn around all the strands about ½″-1″ below the top of the tassel. Then tie and knot your wrap-around strand. Trim the ends of the tassel to even them out.

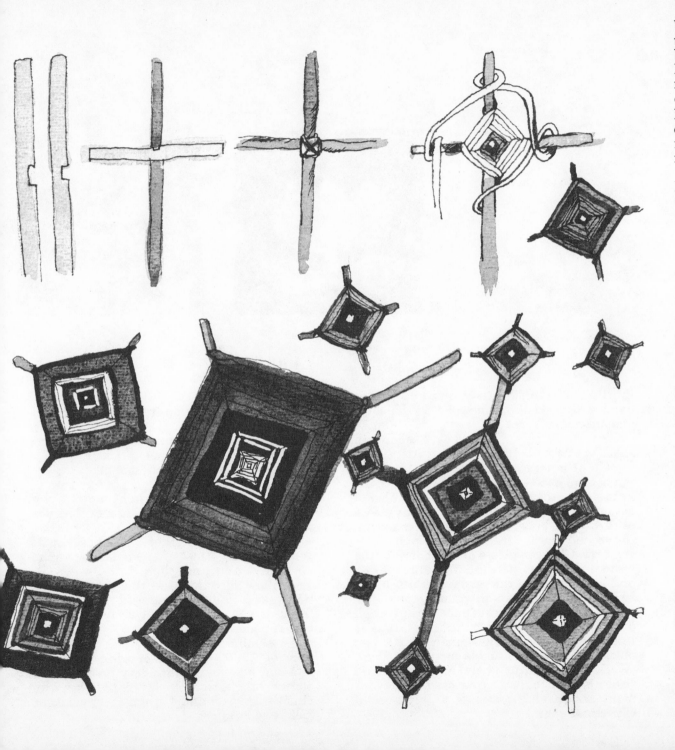

Ojos de Dios (God's Eyes)

When you make God's Eyes, you're practicing an ancient folk art. These yarn symbols are still used today by the Huichol Indians of Mexico in religious festivals. The modern version of this craft can be used to add color and excitement to a room. Make them large or small. Hang them in clusters at different heights, or hang several together from a strip of wood or coat hanger to make a mobile.

Materials:
- assorted colored yarn scraps (not too short)
- ⅛″ dowels, precut into 1′ to 1½′ lengths—cut two of each length—(Have square notches cut out of the dowels' centers ahead of time, as shown.)
- ¹⁄₁₆″ dowels and toothpicks (optional—for smaller God's Eyes)
- thread or embroidery thread (optional)
- white glue and scissors

Glue two dowels of equal lengths together at their notched centers. The two dowels should be perpendicular to each other. Let the glue dry for an hour or more.

Attach one end of a piece of yarn to the center of the cross, where the two dowels join. Wind the yarn forward and completely around one dowel. Bring the yarn back over the top of the dowel, and move on to the next dowel, making a circle of yarn around it. Keep going around each dowel in order. Pull the yarn tightly as you wrap it. As you start going around the cross again, make sure that each length of yarn is right next to the one from the previous round. Don't overlap the wrappings or the lengths of yarn. Use as many colors in your God's Eye as you want. To start a new color, just cut the old color off and tie the new color onto the end of the old color with a double knot.

To make tiny God's Eyes, use toothpicks and thin yarn or embroidery thread. If you want, you can make a God's Eye with three, four, five, or six dowels instead of only two; just make sure that they're evenly spaced when you glue them together.

Christmas Cards Inspired by Latin American Folk Arts

Paper Mola

This is an adaptation of the molas made by the San Blas Indians. A mola is basically a sandwich of colored material.

Materials:
- four pieces of construction paper in four colors
- piece of white construction paper
- nail scissors
- pencil and scrap paper
- white glue
- crayons or marking pens
- small pieces of cardboard

Choose four pieces of construction paper in four different colors. Cut each sheet so that it measures 4" x 5". Place the four sheets on top of each other and cut a tiny notch in each side. (This will help you keep them registered after you start cutting away parts of your design.)

Design your card on scratch paper. Make a design with simple bold shapes the first time you try this technique. (Color your design with three of the same colors you selected for your paper.)

Take the sheet of paper which is the color you did not use in your design. Lightly draw on this first (or top) piece of paper the entire design. Cut out all the parts of the design from this paper.

Place the cut sheet of paper—the top sheet—over the piece of paper which is the most dominant color of your design. Cut out from this second sheet all the design parts except those parts which are the same color as this second sheet of paper.

Place the second cut sheet of paper over the piece of paper which is the second most dominant color in your design. Cut out from this third sheet all the design parts except the parts which are the same color as the sheet you are cutting.

Put the three cut sheets over the fourth sheet but do no cutting on the fourth sheet.

Glue the sheets together by starting with the bottom sheet—the uncut sheet. Place the next sheet—the one with the least number of cutouts— on top of it. Place several tiny pieces of cardboard between the two sheets so that the second one is a fraction of an inch above the first. Glue the pieces of cardboard to the bottom sheet of paper, and then glue the second piece on top of the cardboard bits. Make sure that none of the cardboard pieces show.

Take the third sheet of paper—the second one you cut—and glue it to the first two pieces in the same way. Do the same with the last piece. You now have a mola cut paper design.

Fold the white sheet of construction paper in half to make your card. Glue your mola design to it to create a very special Christmas card.

Cloth Mola

Materials:
- four colored felt scraps (at least 8" square)
- nail scissors
- embroidery thread, pins, needles, and glue
- scratch paper and pencil
- white sheet of construction paper

Design your card on scratch paper. Color your design with three of the same colors you selected for your felt scraps.

Cut four pieces of fabric 8" square. Baste them together to keep them from moving about as you cut and stitch.

Follow directions on this page for cutting your mola. If the material you are using frays as you cut it, turn it under ⅛". Then iron it under.

Assemble the mola according to the directions opposite. Instead of using cardboard bits and glue, use embroidery thread and a blanket stitch. Hold the layers together with pins while you blanket stitch every cut edge. (See page 110.)

Yarn and Beeswax (or Glue) Card

The beeswax technique is the original one used by the Huichol Indians of Mexico.

Yarn and Beeswax Technique

Materials:
- colored yarn scraps
- beeswax (available in sheets at hobby stores)
- cardboard or plywood sheet
- scissors, pencil, and scratch paper
- pin or sharp pointed instrument

Warm the wax in the sun or in a slow oven. You'll want it to be soft enough to hold the yarn you press into it, but not so soft that it liquifies and soaks into the yarn.

Meanwhile, practice sketching a design of fanciful shapes or animals on scratch paper. When you've found one you like,

scratch it into the sheet of beeswax with a pin or sharp pointed instrument. Then press the beeswax onto a sheet of cardboard or plywood, outline the edges of your design with colorful yarn scraps, and fill in the outline shapes with more yarn.

On the back of the cardboard write your Christmas greeting. You will have a truly unique Christmas card.

Yarn and Glue Technique

Materials:
- colored yarn scraps
- white glue
- lightweight cardboard or heavy paper
- scissors, pencil, and scratch paper

Practice sketching a design of fanciful

shapes or animals on scratch paper. When you've found one you like, draw it lightly in pencil onto the piece of cardboard or heavy paper that's the size you want your card to be. (It should be folded in half first, of course, so you can put a message inside it.)

Squeeze a small amount of white glue along the outlines of the basic shapes in your design, starting on the inside of the design and working out. If you want to make a border, too, put a thin line of glue all around the outside edge of your design.

Let the glue set for a few minutes. Then press yarn scraps lightly but firmly along the glue outlines. Be careful not to press so hard that glue saturates the yarn. The glue should touch only the bottom side of the yarn. When you've finished making your outlines, fill in the shapes with more yarn and glue. Let the whole thing dry completely.

More Latin American Christmas Cards

Lovely Christmas cards can also be made using the bark painting technique on page 31.

Or, make a three-dimensional piñata card. Make tiny piñata curls ½" high in assorted colors and glue them onto the top of a folded piece of construction paper. (See page 30.)

Gifts

In keeping with the Latin American spirit, gifts can be made using some of the folk art techniques you used for making the tree ornaments, the crèche, and other room decorations.

For example, you could make a piñata for a friend and fill it with tiny wrapped gifts, individually wrapped fruit, or tiny packets of raisins, granola, and nuts. (See page 28 for instructions on making a piñata.)

Or make a tiny piñata and put a small Ecuadorian Bread-Dough pin inside it. The bread dough can also be used to make earrings and beads for necklaces. (See page 36 for Bread-Dough instructions.)

Use the yarn painting technique to decorate a picture frame or a small mirror glued to a piece of heavy cardboard or plywood. (See page 47 for instructions on Yarn and Beeswax or Glue folk art techniques.)

Make some mola placemats or make a special mola and frame it. (See page 44.)

Make a set of papier-maché puppets to represent the characters in a small book. (See page 40.)

Buy a small book or write one yourself and illustrate it with little bark paintings. Then give the book and the characters to someone special. (See page 31.)

Since most people like to keep a collection of special Christmas ornaments, any of the Christmas ornaments make lovely small gifts for a special friend. You might want to look back at pages 38-43 for some ideas.

Gift Wrapping in a Latin American Spirit

Paper flowers always brighten up a present wrapped in tissue paper. (See page 27.)

Wrap a present in layers of cut tissue-paper banners. Layer the tissue in contrasting colors so that the cut designs stand out. (See page 26.)

Paint butcher paper with brown tempera. Then crumple the paper, let it dry, and iron it. Wrap a present with the dried paper. Make an animal, insect, or plant design on a small piece of brown construction paper and tie onto the gift with colored yarn. Or make several items and glue onto the gift.

Wrap a package with aluminum foil. Draw designs on it with permanent colored marking pens. Tie a colorful yarn pompon around the gift to finish it off. (See page 42.)

syrup from the recipe below.

Syrup

Ingredients:
- 2 c. water
- 2 pieces panocha
- 1 cinnamon stick

Bring 2 cups of water to a boil. Add the panocha and the cinnamon stick. Simmer for 20 minutes at a low temperature. Break buñuelos into little pieces and pour the syrup over them.

Quesadilla

Ingredients:
- 2 c. Masa Harina (found in specialty or gourmet section of some grocery stores)

Latin American Treats to Eat

Buñuelos

Ingredients:
- 2 c. flour
- 2 t. baking powder
- 1 t. salt
- 1½ lb. lard

Sift the dry ingredients together in a large mixing bowl. Add ½ lb. lard. Mix well; then add enough water to make a soft dough. Set aside for twenty minutes.

Divide the dough into balls about the size of a lemon. On a kneading board, roll or pat each dough ball into a circle as large as you want.

Set aside for ten minutes.

Heat 1 lb. lard in a very hot skillet. Drop dough circles into the hot lard. When brown, remove and drain on paper. Serve with the

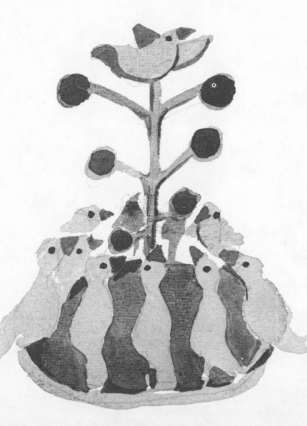

- 1¼ c. water
- 1 t. baking powder
- 1 t. salt
- ½ lb. monterey jack cheese
- ½ lb. lard

Combine the first four ingredients and knead to blend well. (If necessary, add a little more water to make dough hold together.) Shape the dough into twelve balls. To make tortillas, roll out and press each ball between two sheets of waxed paper or pat out by hand to form a 6″ circle.

Cut the cheese into little strips; put a strip of cheese on one side of each tortilla. Fold the tortilla in half. Close the open side with your fingers. Fry in deep hot fat (365°F.) for 10 minutes or until the tortilla is golden brown on both sides. Drain on paper towel. This can also be made with meat instead of cheese. Makes twelve.

A Scandinavian Christmas Celebration

Scandinavian folk arts and designs use the natural textures of fiber, wood, grain, and greenery. Often, a dot or a line is used only to suggest something, not to completely describe it.

A Scandinavian Christmas is rich in the fragrances of evergreens and freshly worked wood. It tastes of almonds. It is simple and yet elegant.

Room Decorations

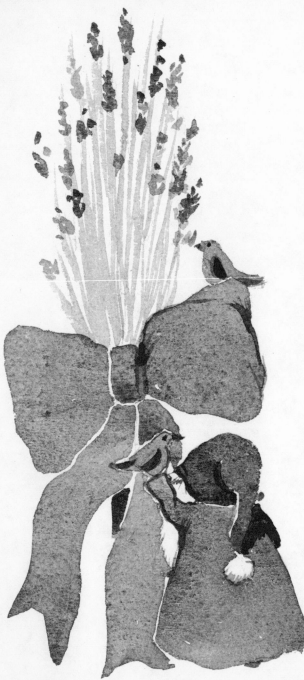

Sheaves of Grain

People in all the Scandinavian countries tie grain into clusters and fasten them to outdoor poles for birds. Today they're often used as a traditional indoor decoration, too.

Materials:
- clusters of any kind of dried grain
- a 36″ long piece of ½″ dowel
- string
- brightly colored ribbon

Tie a bundle of assorted grains around a piece of dowel with a string. Then tie a ribbon around the whole bundle. Stick the pole in the ground where birds can enjoy it. Or, if you like, tie the grain together, decorate it with a ribbon, and pin it to a door inside your house.

Evergreen Advent Wreath

Everyone has one of these in Denmark, and all the markets sell them.

Materials:
- evergreen branches
- straw or styrofoam wreath base
- thin florist's wire
- 6 yards of red ribbon
- four ¾″ x 4″ utility candles and four 3″ nails
- coat hanger or copper wire (optional)
- sphagnum moss (optional)

Tie evergreen branches around the wreath base with florist's wire. (Or, make a 12"-15" ring out of a coat hanger. Tie sphagnum moss or straw around the wire with string until you have a 1"-2" tube. Now begin to tie evergreens around the wreath.)

Stick a nail in the bottom of each candle. Push the candles into the wreath, as shown.

Cut four pieces of red ribbon, each 1 yard long. Tie ribbon around the wreath, placing each yard length in between two candles. Tie the four ribbons together at the top.

Make several small bows out of the extra yards of ribbon to pin around the wreath.

You can also make little red berries out of Ecuadorian Bread-Dough. (See page 36.) Color dough red and roll into ¼" balls. Stick them on wire and insert them into the wreath. Or, pin on some red toadstools. (See page 66.)

Hang your Advent wreath somewhere in your house. On Sunday of the first week of Advent, light one candle. The second Sunday, light two, etc. You may want to sing a Christmas song as you light the candle(s).

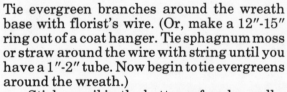

Tomten

In Sweden, a little elf called Tomten delivers gifts to the children. He rides on a goat called a Julbrock.

Materials:
- newspapers
- string or strong red yarn
- one square yard of white or light-colored material—a used baby blanket would be perfect
- a broomstick or a 36″ long piece of 1″ dowel
- the following clothes in children's sizes 4-6: red tights; a blue long-sleeved jersey; a red yarn cap (or make one out of red cloth)
- a skein of white yarn, or ten sheets of white crepe paper, or tissue paper for hair and a beard
- red, black, pink, and blue marking pens
- needle and small amount of thread

Crumple newspaper into a ball about 7″ in diameter. Tie the square of light-colored cloth around it with string or yarn to make a head shape. Stick the dowel or broomstick inside the head as you tighten the string or yarn.

Stuff the red tights and the blue shirt with crumpled newspapers. Tie the ends of the sleeves shut with string or yarn. Stick the broomstick through the neck of the shirt and down through one leg of the stuffed tights.

Tie the shirt around the neck. Tie it again around the waist to hold the tights up.

Make a wig out of white yarn. Cut a skein

of yarn into 18″ long pieces and gather in a bundle. Tie the bundle of 18″ pieces in the middle. Pin it on top of the Tomten's head. Or, cut ten sheets of white tissue or crepe paper into 20″ x 15″ sheets. Fringe both 15″ sides. Tie the stack of paper together and pin it to the Tomten's head.

To make Tomten's face, draw rosy cheeks, a red nose, and two blue eyes with marking pens.

Make a beard out of a bundle of 18″ yarn strands tied in the middle. Cut a few short pieces for a mustache; trim. Pin the beard and mustache to the face.

Stuff the red cap with newspaper and stitch it on Tomten's head. If you don't have a red cap, make one out of red flannel. Cut two triangles of cloth 18″ x 18″ x 10″. Stitch up two sides; hem bottom.

Now your Tomten is ready to be put in a special place where he can preside over the Christmas festivities.

Flags

Another typical Scandinavian decoration for the Christmas season is a string of flags. Make some following the instructions on page 2.

Swedish Peace Tree

Materials:
- cheap unfinished wood lattice (according to the size tree you want)
- flower pot or 1 lb. coffee can
- plaster of paris
- ornaments
- eight apples
- bundle of wheat
- red twine or ribbon

Cut lattice into one long support and four shorter pieces for branches, each one slightly shorter than the last.

Cover the hole in the bottom of the flower pot with tape. Mix plaster of paris according to directions on package. Pour it into the flower pot. Allow it to partially set. Insert the support lattice and hold until it stands alone (3-5 minutes). Tie on branches.

Hang cookies or ornaments from the branches. (See pages 60-68.)

Stick an apple at each end of each branch.

You can make a Swedish Peace Tree in other ways too. For example, make a large one out of cardboard and hang it on a wall. Or make a Peace Tree out of paper, or simply paint one on paper.

Advent Calendar

Materials:
- a piece of fabric 15" x 30" (any kind)
- twenty-four 1" - 1½" metal curtain rings
- fabric scraps (Felt is easiest to work with.)
- scissors, needle, and thread
- scratch paper and pencil

(The piece of fabric is the background for your Advent Calendar. Each ring represents one of the days of December before Christmas.)

Decide where you want to sew the twenty-four rings on your fabric, and then sew them on. Cut the numbers 1-24 out of felt and sew a number under each curtain ring.

Wrap tiny gifts, cookies or candies, nuts or dried fruits into twenty-four small packages. Tie each one to a ring. Open one each day of Advent.

You may want to add some decorative touches to your calendar. If so, on scratch paper, design decorations to cut out of felt for the calendar. Use the sketches as patterns. Cut each pattern out, pin it to a felt scrap, and cut around it. Stitch or glue each decoration you made onto the Advent Calendar.

The Crèche

Danish Acorn Dolls

Materials:
- acorns
- tiny pinecones cut in half
- glue and scissors
- cloth, construction paper, and yarn scraps
- straw for the nativity scene

For each crèche figure, glue an acorn on top of half of a pinecone.

If you are making several figures, glue all the acorns to all the pinecone halves at once and put them aside to dry thoroughly.

Cut triangles out of cloth or paper to use as head coverings. Cut a circular strip of material for each skirt body. Cut arms out of construction paper. Cut beards out of paper or yarn. Wrap a skirt around each pinecone so that the acorn head is above the skirt. Glue the skirt to the pinecone.

For each female crèche figure, glue a triangle around the acorn head to make a kerchief. For each male crèche figure, glue yarn around the head for hair. Attach the arms to the tops of the skirts. Make baby Jesus out of an acorn and a small piece of paper or cloth wrapped and glued around it.

Arrange all of your figures on straw.

Small Stitchery Figures

These can be any size but the larger they are the more stitching and time is required.

Materials:
- scratch paper, pencil, and scissors
- needlepoint canvas, burlap, or cloth with an open weave for stitchery
- needles and embroidery threads or colored yarns
- colored permanent marking pens
- yarn scraps to make a bed for the figures to stand on

Sketch some simple crèche figures on scratch paper. Keep the details very simple. When you've drawn some you like, draw an outline around each one. These will be your patterns. Color each one with marking pens, adding simple clothes, facial features, hair, etc. The colors you use to decorate your patterns should be close to the ones you'll be using when you stitch them. Cut out the patterns, pin each of them on a piece of cloth folded in half, and cut around them. (You'll have a front and a back piece for each figure.)

Color each cloth piece with marking pens according to the designs you drew on the pat-

tern pieces. Then begin stitching each figure. (See page 110 for a stitchery sampler.) Stitch as much or as little of the figure as you can and want to. (The marking pen colors will make it look finished no matter how much stitching you really do!) Color and stitch both the front and back pieces of each figure.

After you've completed both pieces, put the decorated sides together. Sew the two pieces together, leaving the bottom open. Turn the figure inside out and stuff each figure with polyester stuffing. Afterwards, sew the bottom of each figure together.

Place your crèche figures on a bed of yarn.

Scandinavian Christmas Tree Ornaments

The colors used in Scandinavian Christmas ornaments make them truly distinctive. Almost all of the holiday folk arts use red, blue, white, gold, and natural wood or straw colors.

Swedish Horses

These are usually made out of wood but make this version out of cardboard.

Materials:
- cardboard from a grocery box
- a sharp knife to cut the cardboard
- sandpaper
- scratch paper and pencil
- tempera paints and brushes
- clear lacquer or acrylic spray to give horse a shiny coat
- thread

Practice drawing horses on scratch paper.

Keep them simple, concentrating on their outlines. Practice putting some decorative shapes and flowers on them.

When you've drawn a horse you like, cut it out for use as a pattern. Place the pattern on cardboard and trace around it. Cut the horse shape out of the cardboard and sand the rough edges.

Paint both sides of the horse with white tempera. Let it dry completely. Then paint both sides of the horse again, this time with red tempera. In painting the red coat, be careful that you don't loosen the white coat and make the paint turn pink. (Instead of applying the white coat, you could paint two

coats of red paint. It's a good idea to use the white undercoat if you can, however, since the white is more opaque than red and covers any printing that might be on the cardboard.)

When the red paint has thoroughly dried, decorate your horse with hearts, flowers, and greenery. When all the decorations have dried, use a clear lacquer or acrylic spray to give your horse a shiny coat.

Poke a hole through the horse's back and put a piece of thread through the hole for easy hanging.

To decorate a large room, make several large horses. Or, make a set of them in graduated sizes.

Cardboard Yuleman

Materials:
- cardboard from a heavy box
- X-acto knife to cut cardboard
- sandpaper
- tempera paints and brushes
- fake fur, cotton batting, or polyester stuffing
- scratch paper and pencil
- thread

Create a simplified Santa figure on scratch paper. (Scandinavian design is noted for its simplicity. So try to make your design simple in outline in keeping with this Nordic tradition.)

When you've drawn one you like, cut it out for use as a pattern. Place the pattern on cardboard and trace around it. Cut the Santa shape out of the cardboard and sand the rough edges.

Paint the Santa figure following the directions on page 60 for painting on cardboard.

To give the figure texture, make a beard out of fake fur or stuffing material and glue it to the Santa figure.

Poke a hole through Santa's cap and put a piece of thread through the hole for easy hanging.

Julbrock

Julbrock is the Swedish goat that Tomten rides. In Scandinavia, these goats come in all sizes from tiny 1″ goats to sturdy ones 3 feet high.

Crepe Paper Julbrock

Materials:
- golden yellow, red, and white crepe paper (one package of each)
- scissors and glue

Cut the golden yellow crepe paper across the grain into 2″ wide strips. Undo each strip. Using your thumb and index finger, twist the paper into a very tight cord.

Cut the crepe paper cord into about eighty 7″ lengths. Make a bundle of forty pieces for the body; make two bundles of eighteen pieces each for the legs. Make some red cord out of red crepe paper. Wrap it around the body and legs as shown.

Out of white crepe paper, braid cord for the horns. Make two braids, using three pieces of 7″ cord for each braid. Slip these two braids into the body bundle and glue in place. For a tail, make a single braid using three pieces of golden yellow crepe paper cord. Attach this braid to the body bundle.

Add a loop of thread to your Julbrock for easy hanging.

Danish Wood Shaving Ornaments

(to hang on the tree or on evergreen garlands)

Materials:
- 1″ clear pine board or thin veneer strips
- a woodworking plane
- an iron
- rubber bands

If you use the pine board, soak it in water overnight; ten hours ought to be long enough.

Put the board in a vise. Plane along one edge, going from one end to the other.

To hold the curls which emerge from the planing, roll them up and secure them with rubber bands. To flatten them, iron them with a medium-hot iron.

If you use veneer strips, soak them in water to make curls.

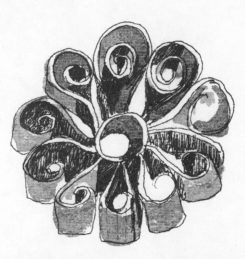

Braided Wreath Ornaments

Materials:
- red, white, and golden yellow crepe paper
- scissors and glue

Cut each color of crepe paper across the grain into 2″ wide strips. Undo each strip. Using your thumb and index finger, twist the paper into a very tight cord.

Make nine 24″ cords out of the golden yellow, red, and white crepe paper. (Make three of each color.) Braid the nine cords together, using groups of three cords at a time. Make each group of three the same color, or use a combination of all three colors in each braid group.

As you finish each braided section, glue the next section to it. When the three sections have been braided and glued together, you will have a long braid. Wrap the braid into a circle with a piece of red crepe cord. Glue in place.

Curl Ornaments

Materials:
- several wood curls
- paper clips
- glue
- needle and thread

After the curls have dried, remove the rubber bands. Play with the curls for a while, arranging them in different combinations and pushing them into various shapes and sizes until you find a design you like. Use paper clips to hold several curls together while deciding on your design. Once you've made up your mind, glue the curls together. Leave the paper clips in until the glue is completely dry. Add a loop of thread to your ornament and hang it from your Christmas tree.

Flat Stars

Materials:
- four 5" long flat wooden strips
- needle and thread
- glue

Place the four wooden strips on top of each other to make an eight-sided cross, as shown. Dab glue in between the places where the strips touch to hold them in place. Let the glue dry completely.

Weave thread over and under alternate strips five to ten times, depending upon the thickness of your thread. Turn the star over and weave back in the other direction. Glue end of string under the weaving.

Add a loop of thread to your star ornament for easy hanging.

Wheat Bundles

Materials:
- dried wheat
- thin red ribbon or red crepe paper twisted into cord
- thread

Tie 5" lengths of wheat together in bundles of ten to twelve pieces each. Tie each bundle with red cord or ribbon. Then tie a piece of thin thread around your bundle for hanging.

Paper Heart Chains

Materials:
- a roll of 2″ adding machine tape or a 10′ length of white butcher paper cut into 2″ strips
- scissors
- transparent tape

Cut the 2″ wide strip into 20″ lengths. Begin to accordion pleat the paper strips. Make the first fold 2″ wide. Make ten 2″ folds so that you have a ten-layer pleat 2″ square.

Draw half a heart on the fold on both sides of the first accordion pleat. Hold the strip together and cut out both half hearts. Do this to several 2″ x 20″ strips. Then tape the strips together with clear tape and drape this chain on your tree.

Kraemmerhus (paper cornucopias)

Materials:
- large sheet of construction paper
- colored marking pens
- scissors, paper clips, and glue

Make a 12″ circle from construction paper. Cut into quarters. Each quarter will make one Kraemmerhus.

Decorate each quarter with marking pens or glue pieces of colored paper to it.

Cut four strips of paper for handles. Decorate each handle, also.

Glue the sides of each quarter together to make a cone. Secure the top of the cone with paper clips until the glue dries. Glue the handles on.

Fill each cone with candies and nuts. Use the handle to hang each cone on the tree.

Papier-Maché Apples and Toadstools

Materials:
- newspaper
- flour and water mixed to pancake batter consistency
- red and white tempera paints
- material for clear acrylic coating
- florist's wire
- green construction paper

Apple

Squeeze ¼ sheet of newspaper into a tight ball. Tear other newspapers into thin strips. Soak the strips in the flour and water mixture and then wrap them around the ball. As you

wrap, squeeze the ball into an apple shape. Continue to cover with newspaper strips until it looks like an apple.

Let your apple dry thoroughly and then paint it red. Spray or brush on a clear acrylic lacquer coating.

Cut a green leaf out of construction paper. Twist one end of the leaf around a 2″ piece of green florist's wire. Secure with glue. Stick the wire into the top of the apple. Dab glue into the hole to hold the leaf in place. Let dry completely and then add a loop of thread for easy hanging.

Toadstool

Squeeze ¼ sheet of newspaper into a ball and flatten one side. This is your toadstool cap.

Make another small newspaper ball and squeeze it into a stubby stem. Wrap both the stem and the cap with newspaper strips soaked in the flour and water mixture. Center the stem in the flat end of the cap and attach with glue. Reinforce the joining with more newspaper strips soaked in the flour and water mixture.

Let dry completely. Then paint your toadstool red with white polka dots.

Attach a loop of thread to the cap of your toadstool for easy hanging.

Bjørn Wiinblad Angels

Wiinblad angels are the exception to the
characteristic simple quality in Nordic design.

Materials:
- construction paper
- scissors
- paint or colored marking pens

Cut 6" to 8" circles from construction paper.
Cut each circle into quarters; each quarter
will be used to make one angel.

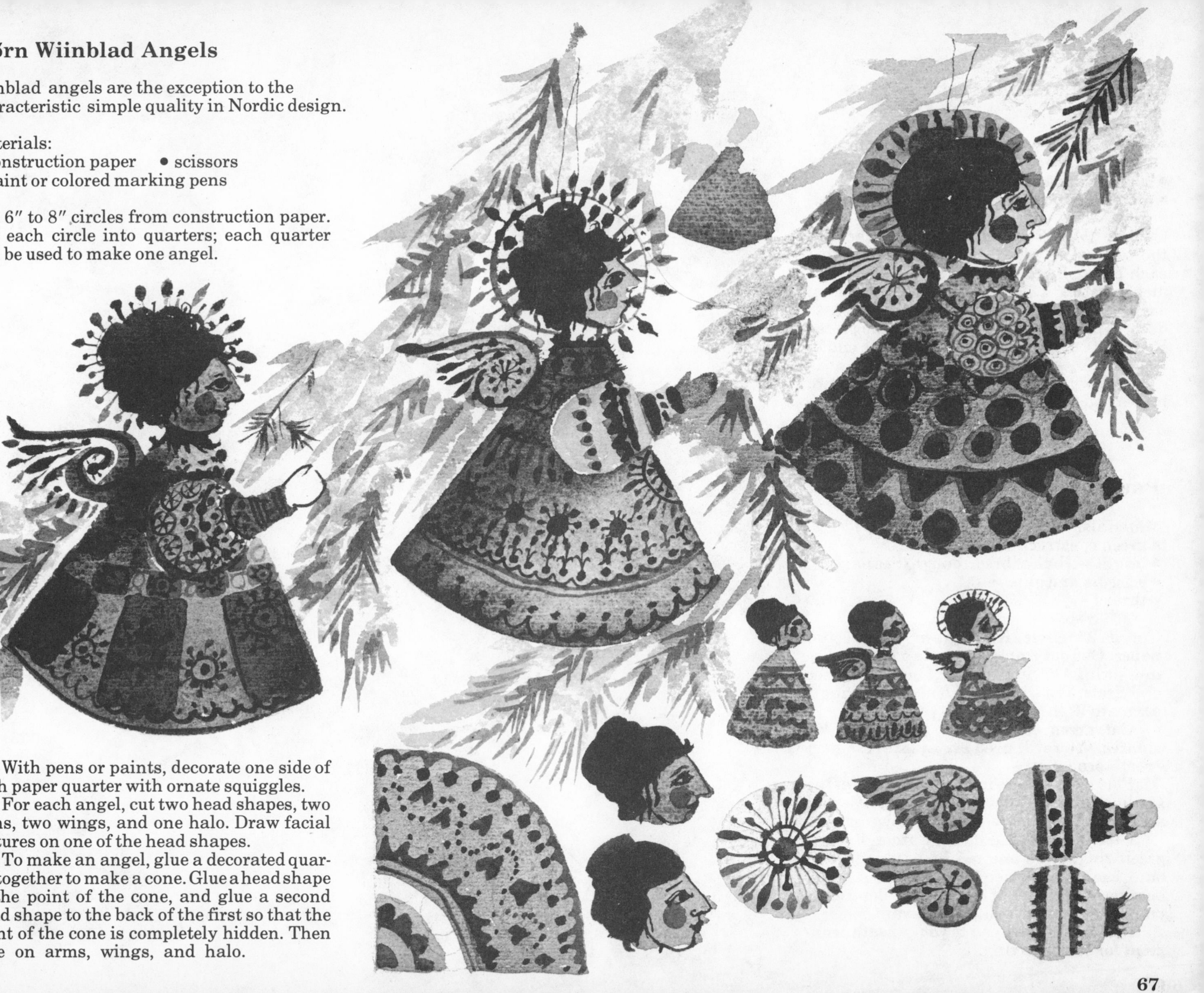

With pens or paints, decorate one side of
each paper quarter with ornate squiggles.

For each angel, cut two head shapes, two
arms, two wings, and one halo. Draw facial
features on one of the head shapes.

To make an angel, glue a decorated quarter together to make a cone. Glue a head shape
to the point of the cone, and glue a second
head shape to the back of the first so that the
point of the cone is completely hidden. Then
glue on arms, wings, and halo.

Woven Danish Heart Baskets

Materials:
- colored construction paper (two colors per heart)
- scissors and ruler
- metallic papers for special hearts (optional)

Cut one 2¼" x 7" piece of paper from each of the two colors of construction paper. Fold each piece of paper in half so that the piece measures 2¼" x 3½". Along the folded edge of each piece, make two cuts ¾" wide and 2¼" deep. (This will give three tails to the piece.) Round off the corners of the opposite end of each piece.

Following the diagram, weave the two pieces together to make a heart basket.

Paper Flower Wreaths

Materials:
- green construction paper
- bright red ball of bread dough (See page 53.)
- scissors and glue
- thread

Cut a 2" circle from green construction paper. Cut out from this circle a smaller one measuring 1½" in diameter. Discard this second circle. You will have left a ½" wide ring or a wreath 2" in diameter.

Cut green construction paper into ¾" squares. (You will need six squares for each wreath ornament.)

Fold each square in half. Draw one of the six illustrated designs on each square. Cut out each design. You now have six flowers.

Glue six unfolded flowers around your green ring. Glue one red bread dough ball onto each of the six flowers. These balls become the centers of the flowers. Bend each point of each flower slightly upward.

Add a loop of thread to your wreath ornament for easy hanging.

Wrapping Ideas

Make some heart chains. (See page 65.) Wrap a gift with brown wrapping paper, and then glue heart chains around it.

Make cord by twisting red crepe paper and then wrap it around brown paper. (See page 63.)

Christmas Cards

Norwegian Rosemaling

Materials:
- construction paper
- tempera paints
- black fine-point marking pen

Practice drawing these folk designs on scratch paper. Once you feel like you can draw them fairly well, draw them once again on a piece of folded construction paper. (This is your card.) Paint the basic shapes you drew on your card. Blend the colors with your fingers. Let dry. Then trace around your design with a black marking pen.

Scandinavian Treats to Eat

Marzipan Candy Sculpture

Ingredients and Materials:
- 1 c. marshmallow cream
- ⅓ c. light corn syrup
- ⅛ t. salt
- 1 t. vanilla
- 6 c. sifted powdered sugar
- 2 pkg. (8 oz.) almond paste (You can find this in the import section of the supermarket.)
- food coloring
- candy thermometer

In a 3-quart pan combine the first four ingredients and 2 cups of powdered sugar. Slowly heat mixture to about 110°F. Crumble the almond paste into the pan. Turn off heat. Keep pan on a warm surface and stir mixture until well blended. Remove from heat.

Turn this mixture onto a board covered with the remaining 4 cups of powdered sugar. Knead in all the sugar and work it until the dough is smooth and holds together.

Divide the dough into several balls. Poke a hole in each ball and put several drops of one color of food coloring into each hole.

Knead the color evenly through the dough. Add more food coloring for a stronger color.

Store marzipan dough in a tightly sealed container in the refrigerator.

Handle the dough like clay. To stick pieces together, dip a finger into water and slightly moisten each piece at the point where you want to join it to another. Sculpture the dough into desired shapes. Finished figures can be brushed with food coloring to brighten or add details. Wrap finished figures in plastic wrap. (Yield: twenty 2″ figures or animals)

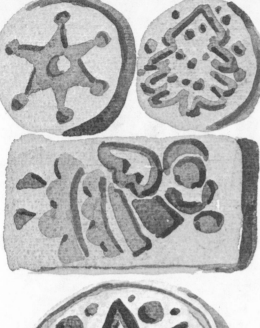

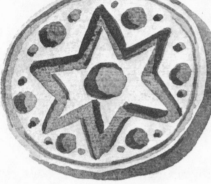

Dry the cookie stamps and fire, or place in oven, according to the instructions on the clay package.

The first time you use the finished cookie stamp, press a lump of cookie dough against the stamp. Remove the dough and flour the stamp. Shake off the flour and begin to use it to make impressions in the following cookie dough:

Cookie Dough

Ingredients:
- 1 c. butter
- ⅓ c. brown sugar, firmly packed
- 3 T. honey
- 2 uncooked egg yolks
- 2 finely mashed hardcooked egg yolks
- ¼ t. almond extract
- ½ t. lemon extract
- 1 t. vanilla
- 4 c. unsifted flour

Blend butter and brown sugar. Add honey and uncooked egg yolks. Mix well. Blend mashed egg yolks into butter and sugar mixture. Add almond and lemon extracts and vanilla. Add flour.

Roll dough onto an ungreased cookie sheet. Press cookie stamps onto dough. Cut away excess dough. Place as many cookies as you can on a sheet. Bake at 275° for 35-45 minutes.

Cookie Stamps

Materials:
- clay or clay substitute
- texture objects (beads, spoons, toothpicks, paper clips)
- clay board and rolling pin

Work clay into a pliable consistency. Roll it flat and smooth. Cut out squares and circles to make 1″-2″ cookie stamps. Using texturing items, draw and press designs into the circles and squares. If you want to write words on the circles or squares, be sure to write them backwards.

Shortbread

Ingredients and Materials:
- ¾ c. sugar
- 1½ c. butter
- 4 c. flour
- several cookie stamps

Cream sugar and butter. Add flour one cup at a time. Mix well. Press onto a cookie sheet. Press stamps into dough. Then cut around stamp to make a rectangular or square cookie. Bake at 325° for 35-40 minutes.

If design disappears while baking, add more flour to the dough next time around.

Rice Porridge
(the Christmas Eve treat)

This wonderful Scandinavian treat is eaten on Christmas Eve. Whoever finds the one —and only one—almond in his or her bowl wins the Marzipan Pig made especially for this occasion.

Ingredients:
- 6 oz. rice
- 1 oz. butter
- 1½ c. water
- 3 c. milk
- ½ t. salt
- 1½ T. Sugar
- cinnamon
- 1-2 c. whipped cream
- 1 (and only 1) almond
- cherry syrup
- a marzipan pig

Rinse rice. Melt half of the butter in an iron pot. Add water and bring to boil. Add rice and boil for 10-15 minutes or until the water has boiled away. Add milk and simmer for 45 minutes, stirring occasionally. Season with salt, cinnamon, and sugar. Add remainder of butter. Cool. Fold in whipped cream. Put in 1 almond.

When you serve this, pour a bit of cherry syrup over it.

St. Lucia Buns (or Lucia cats)

The Swedish celebrate December 13, the Festival of Lights, as the beginning of Christmas. Early in the morning of that day, the oldest daughter in the family dons a white gown and an evergreen wreath crown with five lighted candles. Then she carries a tray of warm rolls to each member of the family and awakens them one by one.

Ingredients:
- 1 c. milk
- 5 grains saffron, if possible
- 2 oz. yeast (or 2 heaping T.)
- 1 egg
- 4 c. flour
- 6 oz. butter
- ¾ c. sugar
- 1 c. raisins
- 25 almonds
- garnish: 1 beaten egg, sugar, and 10 chopped almonds

Warm milk and saffron. Stir yeast into this mixture along with a bit of sugar. Add flour and the egg to the yeast mixture. Mix to a smooth dough. Stir sugar and butter until light and creamy; then work it into dough. Work the raisins into the dough. Let rise for 30 minutes. Scald the almonds and then chop them finely and work them into the dough.

Place dough on floured board and shape into buns. Make a cut on two sides, pulling out the corners, and curl outwards. Place on a buttered baking sheet and let rise for 20 minutes. Brush with the beaten egg and sprinkle with sugar and chopped almonds. Bake in 450° oven until golden brown. Serve warm.

Swedish Pancakes

Ingredients:
- 2 eggs
- ½ t. salt
- 2 T. sugar
- 2 c. milk
- 3 heaping T. flour
- ½ oz. butter for batter
- butter for frying
- fresh berries or other sliced fruits
- whipped cream or topping, chocolate syrup, chopped nuts, chocolate chips, and/or any other treats you want to use to top your pancakes

To make your pancake batter, beat eggs, milk, sugar, and salt together. Put flour in another bowl and gradually add milk mixture to it, beating constantly to prevent lumps. Melt butter and pour it into the batter. Cover and let stand for 2 hours.

Melt butter in a frying pan. Then pour in just enough batter to cover the bottom of the pan. Brown the pancake on one side, then flip it and brown the other side. Place finished pancakes in oven to keep warm.

To serve, place pancake on a plate. Spread with berries or fruits and whipped cream. Then roll up and sprinkle with sugar. Add other toppings, if you like.

For a party, put out bowls of all of the above toppings and let each person make his or her own pancake "sundae."

Danish Kransekage
(Almond Pyramid Cake with Flags)

Ingredients and Materials:
- 2 egg whites
- 16 oz. almond paste
- 1 c. granulated sugar
- frosting glue: 1 egg white, 1 c. powdered sugar, ¼ t. cream of tartar
- ¾ c. powdered sugar
- 1 egg white
- 1½ t. white vinegar
- paper flags glued onto toothpicks (See page 55.)

Beat 2 egg whites slightly. Crumble the almond paste into the egg mixture. Beat thoroughly. Add granulated sugar gradually. Beat until well mixed.

Turn mixture onto a board dusted with powdered sugar. Knead until smooth.

Divide mixture into five balls in graduated sizes. Roll each ball into a rope ½″ in diameter. Make each rope into a ring. Place rings on a cookie sheet. Bake for 25 minutes at 300° F.

To make a frosting glue, mix the listed ingredients. Dab some on each ring as you glue them into a pyramid stack.

Mix ¾ cup powdered sugar, 1 egg white, and the vinegar together until smooth and glossy. Put mixture into a pastry bag or similar frosting decoration device. Press zigzags of frosting over each ring in your pyramid.

Stick flags all over your pyramid cake.

To make a larger cake (and some are very large, 14 layers or more) make more batches of dough. Don't try to double the recipe because it's too difficult to knead the almond paste in large quantities.

Folk Arts for an Early American Christmas Celebration

This celebration isn't an authentic reproduction of Early American Christmas traditions, but rather it is intended as a design for Christmas festivities using American folk arts.

Room Decorations

Paper Quilt Wall Hanging

Folded paper cutouts were often used to create patterns for quilts. The paper cutouts themselves can be turned into a large decorative wall hanging.

Materials:
- colored construction paper
- background material such as butcher paper, large pieces of construction paper taped together, or a piece of fabric
- scissors and glue
- pencil and scratch paper

Make one 12″ square at a time. Pin or glue the squares onto a large background. If you pin the squares, they can be taken down and used again as Christmas cards or as placemats if they're large enough.

If a lot of people are working together on this project in a sort of quilting bee, each individual can be responsible for making a certain number of squares.

The paper quilt could be used as a pattern for a real cloth quilt. This would be a long-term project, of course.

Use some of the cutout designs on this page or make up your own.

Choose a color theme. For a Christmas flavor, you might want to use primarily red, green, and white. Other colors could be used as accents here and there in the design.

3-D Paper Quilt Decorations
(to hang from the ceiling)

Materials:
- colored construction paper (8″-10″ pieces)
- lightweight cardboard or tagboard (8″-10″ pieces)
- scratch paper and pencil
- scissors, glue, and thread

Glue a piece of 8″ construction paper to each side of a piece of 8″ tagboard or cardboard. Do this twice.

Choose another piece of colored construction paper. Fold it in half and make and cut a design pattern for a quilt. (See page 77.) Place your pattern on top of one of your cardboard pieces covered with construction paper. Trace around the pattern. Cut out the design. Do the same thing to your second piece of cardboard covered with construction paper.

For each decoration, you'll need two cardboard cutouts of the same design. Make a slit halfway up to the middle of one; make a slit halfway down to the middle of the other. Slide the two pieces together at these slits.

Make a hole at the top of the decoration. Tie a piece of thread through the hole, and hang your decoration from the ceiling. Make as many decorations as you like. They can be any size, but 8″ to 10″ is suggested.

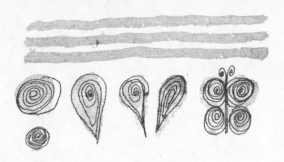

Large Quilled Decorations

Materials:
- colored construction paper or gold or silver foil paper
- scissors and glue
- paper clips and stapler
- paper cutter (a great help in cutting the thin strips of paper required for this project)
- thread
- scratch paper and pencil

Out of construction paper, cut ½" wide strips.

Here are some shapes that you can create by gluing strips of paper together: half of a heart, circle, coil, teardrop, heart.

You can make lots of little shapes in assorted colors and glue them together as you go, making up designs as you glue pieces in place. Or, you can doodle a design on scratch paper. Then decide on the colors you want to use. Cut the paper and begin to create the parts by referring to your sketch plan. Lock separate parts together with paper clips. When your design is completely assembled, remove the clips one at a time as you dab glue onto the paper parts to connect them. Allow your design to dry thoroughly and then remove any remaining clips. Tie a piece of sewing thread around one loop, and hang decoration from the ceiling. Christmas colors can give these ornaments a holiday look.

For especially lovely hangings, use gold or silver foil paper.

A Primitive Christmas Mural

Materials:
- butcher paper
- chalk or pencils
- tempera paints and brushes
- scratch paper

Flatness—a lack of shading and perspective—is the primary characteristic of Early American folk painting. You may want to look at some Early American paintings to get an idea of what this means.

Choose a theme for your mural—such as the Christmas story, Christmas in Early America, or a Christmas celebration with friends. Then practice drawing your picture on scratch paper. In the tradition of Early American folk portraits, you may want to include all of your friends and family members in your mural. Don't forget family pets. If several people are doing the mural together, one person should design the background while the others work on the people and animals. Be sure to share ideas along the way if you're working in a group.

Once you've completed your sketch, draw it on the butcher paper with chalk or pencil.

Then paint in the drawing.

Display your mural somewhere in your home.

Marking-Pen Sampler

In early America, all young girls learned stitchery by making samplers such as these.

Materials:
- a large sheet of colored construction paper
- marking pens (green and red)
- paper and pencil

Using x's in imitation of the cross stitch, draw all the letters of the alphabet on scratch paper. Then try using x's to create decorative figures and a fancy border design. Choose some lines from a Christmas poem or song to put on your sampler. Using red and green pens, make a Christmas sampler on construction paper. Use the alphabet as a border at the top of the sampler. Draw your song or poem beneath the border.

Early American Tree of Life
Advent Calendar

Materials:
- colored construction paper (red, green, and brown)
- scissors and glue
- pencil and scratch paper
- a large sheet of paper to use for a background (optional)
- pins, cellophane tape, masking tape

Practice drawing a tree with lots of branches on scratch paper. When you come up with one

you like, draw it on brown construction paper. (Depending on how big you want your tree to be, you may need to use several pieces of brown paper and tape them together.) Cut out your tree and glue or pin it to the background you've chosen. If you don't have a large piece of background paper, just use the wall and fasten the pieces of your tree to it with clear cellophane tape or masking tape—but be careful so that the tape won't pull paint off the wall!

Then practice drawing leaves, pieces of fruit, blossoms, and heart shapes. When you're happy with your drawings, draw lots of leaves on green construction paper, cut them out, and pin or glue them to your tree shape. Cut out twenty-four pieces of fruit, flowers, or hearts from red construction paper. Number these shapes from 1 to 24. Pin or glue these shapes onto your Advent tree in sequence as each day of Advent passes—one shape for each day.

The Crèche

This section includes directions for making several different types of dolls according to traditional American folk arts. You can use any or all of these dolls as figures in a crèche. For a really interesting crèche, make a few of each type of doll.

Rag Dolls

Materials:
- cloth scraps
- needles and pins
- sewing thread
- scratch paper and pencil
- stuffing material or old nylon stockings
- coat hangers
- yarn scraps
- buttons and other sew-ons
- colored marking pens
- white glue

Decide what figures you want to make for your crèche, and how big you want them to be. Practice drawing them on scratch paper.

When you come up with some figures you like, draw a line all the way around each figure at least ½″ away from it. This will be your cutting line, and will give you room for a seam allowance. Cut out each pattern piece and pin it to a double layer of cloth. Then cut out the fabric pieces around the pattern, following the cutting line. Remove the pattern and pin the right sides of the fabric together. Take a length of coat hanger twice as long as your doll is tall and fold it in half. Wrap the two halves together at the waist.

Wrap another piece of wire around the upper piece of the original wire shape to make arms. Place the wire form inside of the two pinned fabric pieces.

Stitch the cloth pieces together around the edges, leaving a 1½″ slit so that you can add stuffing. Then turn the doll inside out and stuff it, making sure that you don't forget the arms and legs. (It might help to use a piece of wire to push the stuffing into narrow places.) Then stitch up the slit.

On scratch paper, practice drawing some clothes for your doll. You'll probably want to lay your doll down on the scratch paper and trace around it to get some idea of how big its clothes should be. When you come up with a design you like, draw a line about ½″ around it to use for a cutting line, cut it out, and use it for a pattern. Pin the pattern to a double layer of cloth and cut around it on the cutting line. Then either sew the clothing together and dress the doll in it, or glue the clothing to the doll's body. Decorate with buttons and other sew-ons.

Glue stuffing material onto the head for hair, or cut out small lengths of yarn, tie them into a bundle, and sew the bundle onto the doll's head. Add a beard or mustache with stuffing or yarn scraps if you like. Draw on facial features with colored marking pens, or sew on two tiny buttons for eyes. Bend the doll into whatever shape you want it to be in for your crèche.

Apple Dolls

Materials:
- golden delicious apples
- a sharp knife or carving utensil
- toothpicks
- peppercorns, cloves, or tiny dark beads
- coat hangers
- wire cutter
- lemon juice
- non-iodized salt
- watercolors
- clear shellac
- thread or polyester stuffing for hair
- cloth and yarn scraps
- needle, thread, and pins
- toilet paper
- white glue
- buttons and other sew-ons

Peel an apple. Smooth the peeled surface of the apple with your knife. To make a forehead, cut a sloping slice from the top of the apple on the side you've chosen for the face. Create a nose by cutting away the cheek areas so that the nose stands out. Use a toothpick to hollow out the nostrils. With the knife, draw a slit ⅛" deep for a mouth. Cut another line just underneath it. Poke eye holes with a toothpick, and insert beads or peppercorns. Cut lines around the eyes to make wrinkles for an elderly person. Gently smooth the whole apple with the knife edge.

With wire cutters, cut a piece of coat hanger, and insert it through the apple core. Bend the end of the wire that sticks out of the bottom of the apple to keep the apple from slipping off. Dunk the apple in lemon juice and roll it in salt while it is still wet. Then hang the apple up to dry. Choose a place that isn't too hot and that doesn't get direct sunlight. Drying will take 2-3 weeks, depending upon the humidity.

When the apple has dried, use watercolors to paint the face. Then paint or spray the whole apple with clear shellac. Add hair made of stuffing, yarn scraps, or thread.

To make the doll's body, bend a piece of wire into a bobbypin shape as long as you want your doll to be tall. Twist another wire around the body wire for the arms. Wrap the wire shape with toilet paper, using dabs of glue to hold the toilet paper in place. Stick the apple onto the wire.

Make clothing for your apple doll. The basic articles of clothing can be quite simple. (See page 113 for suggestions.) When you have stitched up the sides and hemmed an article of clothing, pin and glue it onto the doll. Stuff toilet paper into the clothing to fill out the figure. Add a hat, apron, or whatever else you want to your basic costume. Decorate your doll's clothes with fabric scraps, buttons, and other sew-ons.

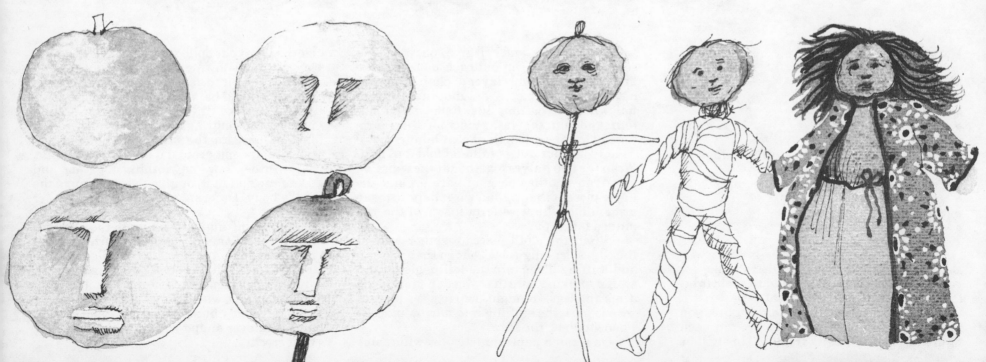

FOLD

Rag Doll Animals

Draw the outlines of some animals you like on scratch paper. Draw each one in profile, so that the head, body shape, and two legs are clearly defined. (Don't worry about the fact that your animals seem to only have two legs—that will be fixed later.) Once you come up with one you like, draw another outline all the way around it ½″ away from the first outline. This will be your cutting line and will give you room for a seam allowance. Cut your animal out, place it on another piece of scratch paper, trace around it, and cut it out again so that you end up with 2 paper cutouts of your animal.

Pin one pattern piece to a double layer of cloth and cut around it. Draw a line across the other paper cutout.

Cut along this line and throw away the top half of the cutout. Place the bottom half—the one with the two legs—on a piece of folded fabric with the long edge up against the fold. Cut around this new pattern piece, but don't cut along the fold. You'll use this funny-looking piece to give your animal four legs instead of two.

With right sides together, pin the two whole animal shapes together along their upper edges and sides. Then unfold the funny-looking shape and pin it to the lower parts of both whole animal pieces, right sides together.

Stitch the animal together, leaving a 1½″ slit in the top for stuffing. Then turn your animal inside out and stuff it with polyester stuffing or pieces of old nylon stockings. (You may need to use a piece of wire or a pencil to push pieces of stuffing down into the legs.) When you've finished stuffing your animal, stitch the opening shut. Give your finished animal yarn hair, a yarn tail, and button eyes, or draw your animal's face on with colored marking pens. Make ears out of small cloth scraps and sew or glue them on where they belong.

When you've made as many stuffed people and animals as you want, arrange them on a bed of small yarn scraps.

Christmas Tree Ornaments

Cardboard Whirligig

Whirligigs are wind toys. They were known as "Sunday toys" because they were small and used in quiet play. Traditionally, most of the figures were soldiers. Use your imagination, and make other figures (Santa, angels, elves) as well as soldiers. Although whirligigs originally were made of wood in the round, this adaptation makes the figures in profile.

Materials:
- pencil and scratch paper
- cardboard
- scissors or knife
- sandpaper
- nail
- tempera paints
- paper clips
- thread

Sketch a profile of the figure you want to make on scratch paper and cut it out. Draw arms on a separate sheet instead of including them on the body. Cut the arms out after making sure that they're the correct size for your figure. Place the figure and the arms on cardboard and trace around them. Cut them out and sand the rough edges of the cardboard. Then paint both sides of the arms and the figure.

With a nail or some other sharp instrument, poke a hole through the upper portion of the figure about where the shoulder should be. Then poke a hole near the top of each arm. Make each hole large enough so that a paper clip can go through it and still leave room for the arms to spin around freely.

Attach the arms to the body with two paper clips. Poke a hole in the head or hat and stick a piece of thread through it so that your whirligig can be hung from a tree branch.

Wax Balls and Figures

Angels and the baby Jesus are typical figures which you might want to make out of newspaper and wax.

Materials:
- newspapers
- flour and water mixed to the consistency of pancake batter
- tempera paints
- wire
- paraffin
- saucepan and warming tray
- soft cloth
- toilet paper
- thread and needle

Wax Balls

Squeeze a sheet of newspaper into a tight ball. Tear other sheets of newspaper into ½″ wide strips. Dip strips into the flour and water mixture. Wrap wet strips around the ball, smoothing as you work until the ball is completely covered and feels sturdy. Then let it dry thoroughly.

Paint it a solid color and let it dry again. Then paint it with some folk paintings, designs, or with patterns of your own.

Stick a wire through the ball. Bend one end so that the ball doesn't fall off the wire. Melt paraffin in an old saucepan on a warming tray. Dip the ball into the melted paraffin, coating it evenly. Let it dry. Dip and coat the ball two more times. When the ball is completely dry, remove the wire. Then rub the ball gently with a soft cloth to bring out a shine. Thread a needle and sew a loop of thread into one end of the ball. Hang it from the tree.

Wax Figures

Make a figure out of wire and wrap with toilet paper. (See page 84.) Tear newspaper into ½″ wide strips, dip the strips in the flour and water mixture, and wrap them around the figure, smoothing as you go. Let the figure dry completely. Then sand the figure and paint it. Dip the figure in wax. (See directions above for the wax ball.)

Quilted Balls

Materials:
- cloth scraps
- polyester stuffing or old nylon stockings
- black embroidery thread
- needles, pins, and scissors

Crazy Quilt Ball

Cut two 3″ circles out of fabric. Put the right sides together. Then stitch the two pieces together, leaving a 1½″ opening for stuffing. Turn right side out, stuff, and stitch the opening shut. Pin tiny scraps of fabric cut in odd shapes onto the stuffed ball. Using a blanket stitch, sew the scraps onto the ball with black embroidery thread. (See page 110.) Attach a thread loop for easy hanging.

Pieced Quilt Ball

Cut several colors of cloth scraps into 2¼″ squares. (¼″ on each square will be a seam allowance.) Sew four squares together into a 4″ x 4″ square. For each ornament, make two squares like this.

Pin a 3½″ paper circle to each square. Cut around the circle pattern to make two quilted circles. Put the two right sides of the quilted circles together. Stitch the circles together, leaving an opening for stuffing. Turn right side out, stuff, and stitch the opening shut.

Attach a thread loop for easy hanging.

Appliqué Ball

Make a plain cloth ball and stuff it according to the instructions given above for the Crazy Quilt Ball. Make a paper cutout within a 3″ circle. (See directions on page 76.) This is your appliqué pattern. Place your pattern on a piece of cloth and cut out your appliqué. Pin the cloth cutout onto the cloth-stuffed circle and blanket stitch it in place. (See page 110 for blanket stitch directions.) Attach a thread loop for easy hanging.

Barn Decorations

It was originally thought that these decorations, called "hex signs," were meant to ward off evil spirits. They're mostly just for looks, though.

Materials:
- colored construction paper—red, green, and white
- scissors, brushes, and glue
- tempera paints—red, green, and white
- yarn or thread

Some traditional designs are shown. You can use these, or make up some of your own, using the basic elements of these traditional designs.

Cut 3″ to 6″ circles out of white construction paper. Then paint the designs on with red or green tempera. Or you can cut the design elements out of red or green paper and glue them onto the white circle. Add a yarn or thread loop to your ornament for hanging.

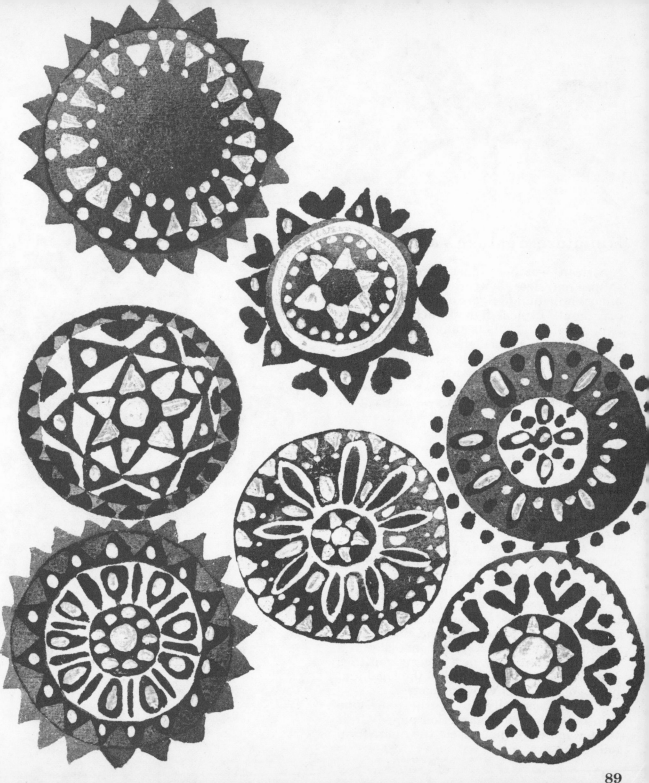

Miniature Weather Vanes

American weather vanes come in many shapes and sizes. A weather vane can have almost any kind of figure on it—as long as it can point! Typical figures include arrows, fish, roosters, Indians, snakes, grasshoppers, livestock, horses, sheep, chickens, pigs, sailors, sea captains, ships, whales, gulls, mermaids, and sea monsters. Sometimes churches have weather vanes, too; these include roosters, fish, and angels blowing on trumpets.

Materials:
• pencil and scratch paper
• scissors
• construction paper
• gold foil (optional)

Draw some figures in profile on scratch paper. When you come up with one you like, draw an arrow somewhere on it if it doesn't have a strong directional element, such as an arm or a head pointing in one direction.

Cut out your drawing and use it as a pattern. Place your pattern on colored construction paper. Trace around it and cut out your weather vane figure. Cut out details as you would if you were making a paper cutout. (See page 76.) Then tie a thread to the head and hang your weather vane from a tree.

For an especially nice weather vane, glue gold foil onto the construction paper. Or, if the foil is heavy enough, cut the figure from foil in the first place.

Wood Turnings

Materials:
- scraps from a local wood turner's
- wood spools
- wood beads
- glue
- tempera paints and brushes
- clear acrylic spray

Try to make figures out of assorted wood turning scraps, spools, and beads by stacking them into figures and shapes. Glue them together with white glue. Let them dry overnight. Paint with tempera. Spray with clear acrylic. (You might want to paint some with folk designs.) Attach a thread loop to each shape for easy hanging.

Quilled Ornament

These are smaller versions of the decorations found on page 79.

Materials:
- colored construction paper
- scissors
- toothpicks
- white glue
- waxed paper
- thread

Cut strips of paper ¼" wide and 12" long. Roll each strip on a toothpick to make a curl. Make up lots of curls. Glue some of these curls into the shapes shown. Arrange other shapes on a piece of waxed paper. When you find an arrangement you like, glue all the little shapes together with dabs of white glue. Let your ornament dry. Then tie a thread loop through one of the curls for easy hanging.

Christmas Cards Inspired by American Folk Arts

Cut Paper and Watercolor Card

Materials:
- white watercolor paper or white construction paper 4¼″ x 11″
- colored construction paper 8½″ x 11″
- watercolors and brushes
- pencil and scratch paper
- scissors and glue
- iron

Fold a piece of white paper in half. Sketch a Christmas scene on one half; for example, people around a tree, an angel, a crèche, or a dinner scene. (Remember, you are drawing only half of your finished picture.) Cut away the background, being careful to keep each figure attached to the next one. Be especially careful to leave some of the folded edge uncut.

Unfold paper. Iron it flat. Paint in the details. Fold a piece of colored construction paper in half to make your Christmas card. Glue your cut paper to the front of the card.

Fractur Painting

Fractur is a decorative folk art brought to the U.S. by the German immigrants. It's said to have come from a sixteenth century typeface that imitated medieval calligraphy. Fractur is a form of illumination used to embellish important family records such as birth and marriage certificates. Penmanship samples for students to copy were also popular. For special occasions, "presentation pieces" were made for friends.

Materials:
- watercolor paper
- watercolors, brushes, and pens
- scratch paper
- drawing pen and ink

On scratch paper, practice drawing some of the fractur elements shown. Experiment with fancy lines and decorative strokes. When you're comfortable with the technique, make up a Christian message.

Fold a piece of watercolor paper in half. Decorate outside with watercolor designs; write your message on the inside in ink, using fractur design elements.

American Treats to Eat

Sugarplums

Ingredients:
- ½ lb. dried apricots
- ½ lb. dried pitted prunes
- ½ lb. dried figs
- 3 c. sugar
- 2 c. water
- ¼ t. cream of tartar
- 2 T. butter
- sugar for rolling the fruit in

Place dried fruits in a strainer and steam over boiling water until they're soft and plump (about 15 minutes). Cover with foil.

Make a fondant stuffing for your sugarplums as follows: mix sugar, water, and cream of tartar in a deep saucepan. Stir until sugar dissolves. Cover and cook at medium setting for 3 minutes. Uncover and place a candy thermometer in the mixture. Cook without stirring until the thermometer reads 239°.

Pour the thick syrup onto a large smooth surface. Let it stand 30 minutes until it begins to set and become thick and white.

With a spatula, scrape the mixture from one side to the other, smoothing it back and forth. As you move it, it will thicken and turn white. When this happens, knead it for 5 minutes until it becomes very smooth. Cut the butter into bits and knead it into the warm fondant.

Dust your hands with cornstarch or flour and roll the fondant into ½″ balls. Stuff each ball into a piece of steamed fruit. Roll each piece of fruit in sugar, and then wrap it in plastic wrap. Store in refrigerator.

Suet Plum Pudding

Ingredients:
- 1 c. raisins
- 1 c. molasses
- 1 egg
- 2 t. cinnamon
- pinch salt
- 1 c. suet, chopped fine
- 1 c. milk
- 3½ c. flour
- 1 t. cloves
- 1 t. nutmeg
- 1 t. soda

Combine ingredients. Pour into a pudding mold placed over a pan of water. Boil over medium heat for 3 hours.

Sugar Cookies

Ingredients:
- ½ c. butter
- 1 c. sugar
- 1 T. milk
- 2 eggs, well beaten
- 1 t. vanilla
- ½ t. salt
- 2 t. baking powder
- 1½ c. sifted flour

Cream butter. Add sugar, milk, eggs, and vanilla. Sift together 1 cup flour, the baking powder and the salt. Add to butter and egg mixture. Slowly add more flour until the dough reaches the consistency at which it can be rolled out—not too sticky, yet not too dry. Chill the dough for 1 hour.

Roll out the dough. Cut it with cookie cutters. Place the cookies on lightly greased cookie sheets. Bake for 8 minutes at 375°. This recipe makes thirty 3″ cookies.

Johnny Cakes

These delicious cakes come from the American Indians and are really called Shawnee cakes; but *Shawnee* sounds so much like *Johnny* that somebody confused the two words a long time ago!

Ingredients:
- 2 c. milk
- 6 c. cornmeal
- 1 c. flour
- 1 t. salt
- ½ c. molasses or honey

Scald the milk in a saucepan. Add the remaining ingredients to the milk. The mixture should form a stiff batter. Spread the batter onto a lightly greased baking sheet. Bake at 350° until brown.

A Gingerbread Christmas — Folk Arts from the Kitchen — A Completely Edible Celebration

What's the cultural significance of this celebration? It doesn't have any! A part of every celebration is just plain fun. This is the just plain fun part of this book. It can ruin your teeth and make you fat. It's the delicious part that every Christmas celebration should have.

This Christmas celebration in and from the kitchen not only looks good, but it tastes delicious too. All of these projects are made in the kitchen, and almost every one can be eaten. Some can even be nibbled during production.

Christmas Cookie Crèche

Make the cookie dough the night before. The recipe makes twelve 6″ crèche cookies.

Cookie Dough

Ingredients:
- 3½ c. sifted all-purpose flour
- ½ t. salt
- 1 t. soda
- 1 t. ginger
- 2 t. cinnamon
- ½ c. butter
- ½ c. packed brown sugar
- ½ c. dark molasses
- ½ c. buttermilk
- ½ t. vinegar

Materials:
- scratch paper and pencil
- lightweight cardboard
- scissors
- clear plastic spray (optional)
- small brushes
- evergreen or hay

Sift half (1¾ c.) of the flour with salt, soda, ginger, and cinnamon

In a separate bowl, cream butter and brown sugar until fluffy. Blend in molasses, and then add the flour mixture.

Mix buttermilk and vinegar. Add this mixture alternately with the rest of the flour to the molasses mixture. Cover and refrigerate the dough overnight.

The next day, preheat the oven to 375°. Grease cookie sheets.

In the meantime, draw some crèche figures 5″ to 6″ high. Keep the basic shapes

simple. You can add fancy details later with frosting. When you've drawn some figures you like, cut them out and use them as patterns. Place them on cardboard and cut around them. These cardboard shapes will be your "cookie cutter" patterns.

Divide the chilled dough into four balls. Roll out one ball on a lightly floured surface until it's about ¼″ thick. Place the cardboard patterns on the dough. With a sharp knife, cut around the patterns. Move the cookies with a spatula to the greased cookie sheets.

Bake for 10 minutes and cool overnight.

Icing for painting cookies

Ingredients:
• 2 egg whites
• 2 c. powdered sugar
• ¼ t. vanilla
• ¼ t. cream of tartar
• food coloring

Beat the first four ingredients at high speed until icing holds its shape.

Then divide the icing into several bowls depending on how many colors you want. Add food coloring to the icing in the bowls; leave some of it white. Paint the cookies with brushes dipped in icing. Paint one color at a time on all the cookies. Let the icing dry thoroughly before adding more details on top of an iced area. If you plan to keep the cookies instead of eating them, glue the cardboard patterns to the backs of them and spray them with clear plastic.

Arrange the cookies in a bed of evergreen or hay to make your crèche.

Christmas Tree Ornaments

Gingerbread Sculpture

Materials:
- gingerbread dough
- honey dough
- garlic press and toothpicks

Gingerbread Dough

Ingredients:
- 1½ c. molasses
- ⅓ c. vegetable shortening
- 1 c. light brown sugar, firmly packed
- ⅔ c. water
- 6 c. all-purpose flour
- 2 t. soda
- 1 t. salt
- ½ t. cinnamon
- ¼ t. nutmeg
- ¼ t. ginger

Cream the first three ingredients. Add ⅔ cup water and mix thoroughly. Sift together the remaining ingredients.

Add flour mixture one third at a time to

the molasses mixture. Beat thoroughly. Add more flour if the dough is sticky. Roll out to ¼″ thick, and shape the dough with your hands as you would bread dough or clay. Use honey dough for contrast. Bake on waxed paper on a cookie sheet for 10 minutes at 350°. Baking time will vary with the thickness of the dough.

Honey Dough

Ingredients:
- ⅓ c. vegetable shortening
- ⅓ c. sugar
- 1 egg
- ⅔ c. honey
- 1 t. lemon extract
- 3 c. all-purpose flour
- 1 t. soda
- 1 t. salt

Blend the first five ingredients until creamy. Sift together the flour, soda, and salt.

Add dry ingredients to the creamed mixture gradually. Add more flour if the dough is too sticky. Roll out dough to ¼″ thickness and shape it with your hands. Use with dark

gingerbread dough for contrast. Bake on waxed paper on a cookie sheet for 10 minutes at 350°. Baking time will vary with the thickness of the dough.

Stained Glass Cookies

Materials:
- gingerbread dough
- brightly colored hard candies
- hammer to crush candies into small lumps
- thread

Crush candies and sort into small bowls according to colors.

Roll the cookie dough into thin ropes. Press the ropes into outline shapes, such as angels, animals, windows, stars. Put the ropes directly onto waxed paper on a cookie sheet. Bake for 5 minutes at 350°. Remove from oven and sprinkle the crushed candies into the open spaces. Return the cookies to the oven for 3-5 minutes. Then remove from oven and cool. Peel off waxed paper. Tie a thread through each cookie and hang it from the tree.

Pretzel Ornaments

Materials:
- assorted pretzels (in all the sizes and shapes you can find)
- frosting glue (1 c. powdered sugar and 1 egg white)
- assorted dry cereals
- assorted small crackers
- waxed paper
- thread

Work on a piece of waxed paper. Put pretzels, dry cereals, and crackers out on a tray so that you can see all the shapes and sizes. Mix the frosting glue in a bowl. Arrange the pretzels in fanciful combinations. When you see one that you like, glue the combination together with frosting. Let the ornament dry for several hours; then gently lift it off the waxed paper. Tie a piece of thread to the ornament and hang it from the tree.

102

Molded Sugar Balls
with Tiny Scenes

These scenes are created from people and animals made from gingerbread dough on page 100.

Ingredients and Materials:
- 1 egg white
- 2 c. sugar
- food coloring
- plastic hosiery containers or plastic ball mold
- frosting glue (1 c. powdered sugar and 1 egg white)
- tiny gingerbread people and animals to glue into the balls (See recipe on page 100.) Paint the tiny cookies with icing recipe on page 99.
- skewer
- thread

Mix 2 cups granulated sugar with 1 egg white. Color it with a few drops of food coloring. Knead color into sugar.

Pack the colored sugar mixture into your plastic mold. Press it in firmly. With a spoon scoop out the center leaving a ½″ shell. Place a spatula over the top of the mold. Gently turn the mold over and tap it gently to unmold the sugar. Slide the sugar onto a cookie sheet. If it breaks, start again with the same sugar. The first few may break until you get the hang of it.

After you've made several sugar shells, bake them for 10 minutes at 200°. Remove them from the oven, scrape away loose sugar, and bake for 10 more minutes. Then let them cool.

Heat a skewer in a flame, and then stick it through the top of the ball to make a hole for threading. Decorate the ball with frosting paint and tiny gingerbread folk that you have painted. Glue them inside the ball with frosting glue.

Attach a thread hanger and hang your ornament from the tree.

Popcorn Balls and Wreaths

Ingredients and Materials:
- popcorn
- 1¼ c. sugar
- ½ c. light corn syrup
- ½ c. water
- 3 T. butter
- needle and string
- waxed paper

Pop corn and keep it warm. Mix sugar with light corn syrup, water, and butter in a saucepan. Mix until dissolved. Cook without stirring to 270°. Use a candy thermometer so you can tell when the proper temperature is reached. Pour the syrup over the warm popcorn and form by hand into balls. After the balls are dry, attach a thread loop to each ball to hang it to the tree.

For wreaths, string popcorn and tie to make a circle. Dip the circle into syrup and place it on waxed paper to dry. Hang these chains on the tree.

Wrapping Paper Made in the Kitchen

Cookie Cutter Prints

Materials:
- thick tempera paints in flat dishes
- tissue paper, butcher paper, or brown paper bags
- assorted cookie cutters

Dip cookie cutters into flat dishes of tempera and transfer the designs onto tissue paper, butcher paper, or brown paper bag. Print in repeating designs of lines, or alternate several colors and shapes.

Vegetable Prints

Materials:
- tempera paints in flat dishes
- potato or oranges, lemons, artichokes, carrots
- sharp knife
- tissue paper
- scratch paper and pencil

Draw simple designs on scratch paper. Then cut a potato in half and draw your design on the potato with a pencil. Cut away the outside of the design with a sharp knife so that your design stands ⅛″ above the rest of the potato. Dip potato into tempera paint and stamp it onto tissue paper.

Or, use oranges, lemons, artichokes, or carrots instead of a potato. You won't need to make a design because each of these has its own design. Just cut them in half and use them to print paint onto tissue paper.

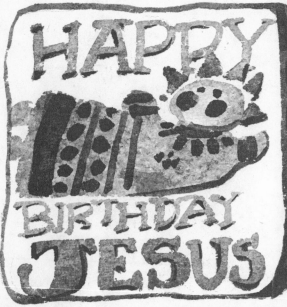

Cooked Christmas Cards

Painted Shortbread Cookie Cards

Ingredients and Materials:
- 2 c. butter
- 2 c. sugar
- 2 t. vanilla
- 5 c. unsifted flour
- 6-7 T. warm water
- 1½ lb. powdered sugar
- food coloring
- brushes

Cream butter, sugar, and vanilla. Add flour and mix until dough holds together. Roll onto floured surface and cut into two dozen 4″ squares or balls. Bake at 300° for 25-30 minutes or until dough is pale yellow.

Mix water and powdered sugar until smooth. Paint it over cookies so that they're covered with a smooth icing glaze. Let dry overnight.

With brushes dipped in undiluted food coloring, paint designs, pictures, and messages on your shortbread cookie cards.

Gumdrop Cards

Materials:
- colored construction paper
- assorted gumdrops and candies
- frosting glue (1 c. powdered sugar and 1 egg white)
- nontoxic marking pens and pencil

Draw a design or picture on a folded piece of construction paper. Color the design with nontoxic marking pens. Decorate further by gluing sliced gumdrops onto the design or picture with frosting glue. Send the card to a friend suggesting that she or he peel off the candies and eat them.

A Stitchery Sampler

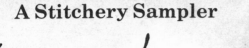

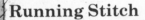

Running Stitch

Stem Outline

For fine lines, work left to right, inserting needle a short distance to the right and bringing to left at a slight angle. For stem, keep thread below needle. For outline, keep thread above needle.

Long and Short Stitch

Work as for satin stitches, staggering long and short stitches. Shade with this stitch.

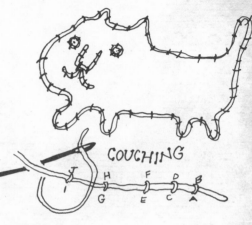

COUCHING

Couching

Use to tack down lines of yarn or for lines and outlines. Place thread along line, tacking down with small, even stitches. Use also to secure long satin stitches.

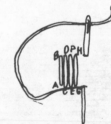

PADDED SATIN STITCH

Satin Stitch

Use to cover small background areas. Bring needle up at one edge; insert at opposite edge; return to starting edge, carrying needle under fabric.

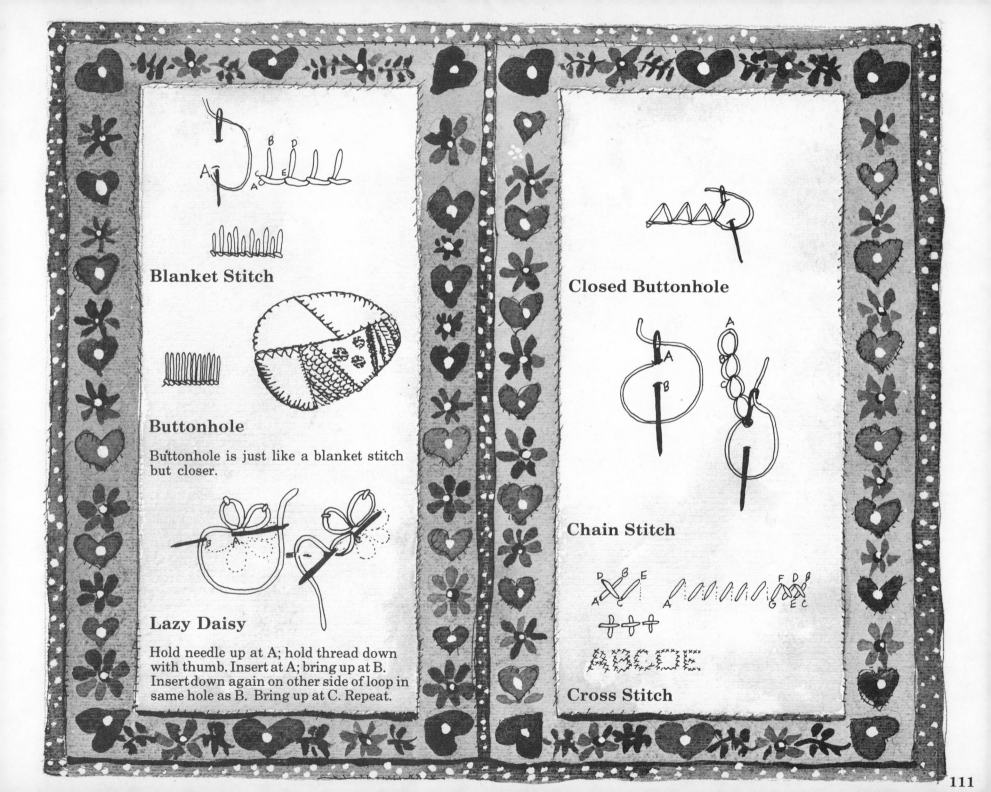

Blanket Stitch

Buttonhole

Buttonhole is just like a blanket stitch but closer.

Lazy Daisy

Hold needle up at A; hold thread down with thumb. Insert at A; bring up at B. Insert down again on other side of loop in same hole as B. Bring up at C. Repeat.

Closed Buttonhole

Chain Stitch

Cross Stitch

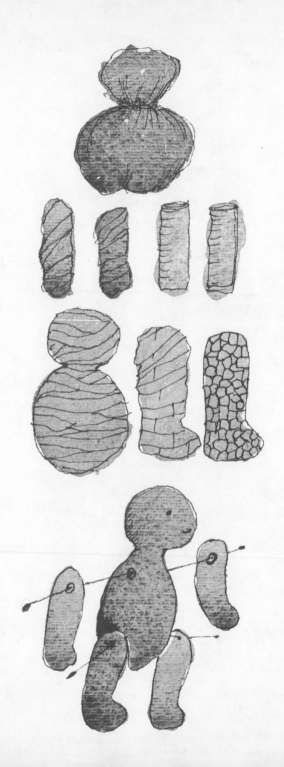

Papier-Maché

Instructions for Making Basic Papier-Maché Figures and Puppets

Materials:
- brown bags in assorted sizes
- newspapers
- flour and water mixed to the consistency of pancake batter or liquid starch
- masking tape
- tempera paints and brushes
- white paper towels
- shredded construction paper
- hammer and a long nail
- coat hanger wire and wire cutters

To make a figure, choose a brown bag that's as long as you want your figure to be high.

Crumple newspapers and stuff them into the bag. Form the bag into a head and body shape by wrapping tape around the neck.

Mix flour and water to a consistency like pancake batter. (Or use liquid starch.) Tear newspapers into 1″ strips. Dip newspaper strips into the flour and water mixture (or into the liquid starch) and wrap them around the paper bag, pressing them down to remove any lumps.

Cut arm shapes out of several layers of newspaper. Wrap shapes with strips of flour-water soaked newspaper. Pat and press each piece into its desired shape. Use strips of newspaper to fasten the arms onto the body—wrap strips around the body and over the ends of the arms, then wrap strips up around the arms and then around the body again. Do this several times until the arms are securely in place.

Or, roll newspapers into ½″ thick rolls. Cut them into 2″-3″ lengths. (These will be the arms and legs of your doll.) Wrap them with newspaper strips dipped in flour and water. Press and bend them into the arm and leg shapes you want. With a nail, hammer a hole through each arm and leg, and then hammer holes through the upper and lower parts of the torso, as shown. Put lengths of wire through the holes and attach the arms and legs to the body.

Cover the whole figure—head, body, and arms—with three layers of newspaper strips. Then tear paper towels into ½″ pieces, dip them into the flour and water mixture, and press them all over the figure. Cover the entire figure until it's smooth. Let dry thoroughly. Then paint with tempera paint in a skin color. Allow paint to dry thoroughly before painting details on your figures or animals.

Making Doll Clothes

Index

286

23 9 163